Nineteen Hundreds Overview

- The dawn of the Golden Age came in 1900. People around the world looked for growth and opportunity in the new century, and many believed that their opportunities would come in America. Throughout the decade, millions of immigrants flocked to the United States in search of the "American Dream." Some found it while others lived their lives in pursuit of it, but always there remained the hope that hard work and determination would lead to a golden future.

- Queen Victoria died in 1901, marking the end of the Victorian Age. For 63 years she had been the symbol of the British Empire, of which the British said with pride, "The sun never sets on the Empire."

- Colonies and territories came with a price. Sometimes the citizens did not wish to be ruled by a country overseas, and turmoil ensued. The rush for power throughout Europe and Africa served, in part, as a catalyst for the great war of the next decade. The Boxer Rebellion, the Boer War, the Russo-Japanese War, and revolution in Russia added to the growing world turmoil, as did riots and rebellions in Spain, France, Turkey, the Gold Coast, and Tanganyika.

- As a result of the Spanish-American War, the United States gained control of the former Spanish colonies of Guam, Cuba, and Puerto Rico. A treaty with France and Great Britain created American Samoa in the South Pacific, and Hawaii was annexed.

- Oklahoma became a state in 1907, bringing the number to 46.

- Natural disasters struck around the globe. Mt. Pelee in the Caribbean and Mt. Vesuvius in Italy both erupted with tragic results. Italy, South America, and the United States all saw earthquakes that cost millions in damages and destroyed thousands of lives.

- President McKinley was assassinated near the beginning of the decade. Theodore Roosevelt, the former Rough Rider and Vice President, took the helm for most of the decade. Roosevelt fought hard to keep big business in check. He is perhaps most popularly remembered today for his namesake, the Teddy bear.

- In 1907, Roosevelt sent "the Great White Fleet" of American naval ships around the world to demonstrate American strength.

- The International Ladies Garment Workers Union began in 1900. The Industrial Workers of the World, a militant labor union sometimes called "Wobblies," was founded in 1905.

- Industry and invention revolutionized the world. Earlier inventions such as the telephone and the electric light came into widespread use. Automobiles began to replace bicycles and horse-drawn vehicles, and wireless communications connected the world in new ways.

- Lyman Frank Baum published *The Wonderful Wizard of Oz* in 1900. The first of 14 books about Oz, it has become a children's classic.

- Cinema moved from vaudeville houses to small theaters, called nickelodeons. *The Great Train Robbery* set the pace for melodramas, and Georges Melies of France experimented with special effects in *A Trip to the Moon*. Film censorship began in 1909.

- The Wright brothers brought flight to the world with their successful ride at Kittyhawk, North Carolina.

- The age of the automobile came under full swing as Henry Ford introduced the mass-produced Model T Ford.

- At the close of the decade, Peary and Henson became the first people to reach the North Pole, decreasing the amount of unexplored land on the planet. Little did the average person think that the close of the new century would bring exploration beyond the planet and throughout the galaxy.

Suffragettes

Throughout the nineteenth century, groups of women organized and demonstrated to reform education, establish rights to property, and provide opportunities for certain previously unattainable professions (such as medicine) for women. By the time the twentieth century dawned, they had begun to focus their goals on the right to vote, also known as *suffrage*. These women reformers became known as suffragettes.

There was strong resistance to the movement throughout the country and, in fact, the Western world. Women everywhere were fighting for the right to vote, but tradition, prejudice, and even a sense in some of moral righteousness proved difficult to combat. However, the suffragettes persisted. They themselves sometimes disagreed on tactics; however, they strongly believed that all methods of reform should be strictly legal so as to combat any suggestion that women are emotionally volatile and therefore incompetent to vote.

The National American Woman Suffrage Association (NAWSA) was highly active at this time. It held conventions, waged state-by-state campaigns, and distributed literature to bring about change. Suffragettes followed the example of women in Britain who were fighting for the vote and held parades and outdoor speeches on a regular basis. Eventually, the cause realized that it needed to appeal to two factions of women, both the social reformers and those seeking equal rights. The social reformers realized that they needed the vote to bring about change, and college-educated, working, and career-minded women were natural supporters for equal rights. The union of the two groups proved successful. Little by little, individual states began to give the vote to women, though it would not be until the close of another decade that the United States Constitution was amended to give women the vote.

Suggested Activities

Research Research their lives and influences on the suffrage movement: Alice Paul, Lady Astor, Lucy Stone, Henry Blackwell, Susan B. Anthony, Elizabeth Cady Stanton.

Voting and the Sexes Examine the differences in voting results when only males vote, when only females vote, and when both sexes vote. Conduct class votes on various subjects. Have all voters mark their ballots M for male or F for female, or provide differently colored ballots to each sex. Discuss the results and differences, if any. Consider a wide variety of topics for voting.

NAWSA The NAWSA was formed from the combination of the National Woman Suffrage Association (NWSA) and the American Woman Suffrage Association (AWSA). Research to find out more about these organizations and their dynamic founders. How did the two differ from one another, and why did they decide to join forces?

The Graduate

Helen Adams Keller was born in 1880 normal and healthy, but at age one and one-half she suffered what the doctor called "acute congestion of the stomach and brain." The illness destroyed her sight and hearing. For nearly five years afterwards, Keller was almost completely cut off from the rest of the world, unable to speak and communicating only through giggles and choked screams.

At the advice of Alexander Graham Bell, Keller's father wrote to the Perkins Institution for the Blind in Boston. Just before Keller was seven, Anne Mansfield Sullivan arrived to undertake her teaching. Together they developed a way to communicate, Sullivan spelling into the hand of Keller manually. Once the girl understood the method, her learning was rapid. Within three years, Keller was a fluent reader and writer of Braille, the alphabet of the blind.

Helen Keller

At age ten, Keller took lessons from a teacher of the deaf to learn how to speak. At sixteen, she went to preparatory school and continued her studies at Radcliffe College. Anne Sullivan attended classes with her as her interpreter. In 1904, the impossible happened. The blind and deaf young woman, once entirely unable to communicate, graduated from college—with honors.

Helen Keller went on to be a noted author (her books have been translated into over fifty languages) and lecturer. Communication became her gift to the world. She worked for the remainder of her life to help the blind and deaf, doing such things as starting the Helen Keller Endowment Fund and working with soldiers in World War II who had been blinded in battle.

Some of Keller's books include *The Story of My Life* (1902), *Optimism* (1903), *The World I Live In* (1908), and *Teacher* (1955) which is the story of Anne Sullivan. Helen Keller's early life has been immortalized in the award-winning play *The Miracle Worker* (1959) and the motion picture of the same name.

Suggested Activities

Braille Below you will find the Braille alphabet as it appears visually, along with four words made with their own dot code. In reality, the dots are raised indentations on paper. Use the system of dots as you see it to write a message. Have a classmate translate your work.

A	B	C	D	E	F	G	H	I	J

K	L	M	N	O	P	Q	R	S	T

U	V	W	X	Y	Z	and	of	the	with

College Helen Keller was able to attend and graduate from college, but it is unlikely that she would have been able to do so without the help of Anne Sullivan. Do some investigating to find out what help is available in colleges today for people with special needs.

Flight

At the turn of the century, very few believed that flight was possible in a heavier-than-air machine. Two of the few who did believe were Wilbur and Orville Wright. Wilbur Wright was born in 1867 in Indiana, and Orville was born four years later in Ohio. As children the two were fascinated by mechanics and even earned small amounts of money by selling homemade mechanical toys. Both went to school, but neither received a high school diploma. When they grew up, Orville built a printing press and started a printing business, developing a weekly newspaper which Wilbur edited. Next, they tried their hands at renting and selling bicycles, and finally they began to manufacture the bikes themselves.

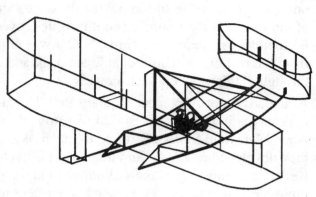

In 1896 the brothers read about the death of a pioneer glider named Otto Lilienthal, and his work sparked their interest. They started to read everything available on aeronautics and soon became as expert on the subject as any pioneer could be. The Wrights then contacted the National Weather Bureau to determine the best place to carry out their experiments with flight. The Bureau advised them to try a narrow strip of sandy land called Kill Devil Hill near Kittyhawk, North Carolina. In 1900, they tested a glider that could hold a person, and in 1901 they tried again with a larger glider. Neither glider could lift as they had hoped, although they did achieve some success in controlling balance.

The Wright brothers felt confident that flight was possible; therefore, they theorized that previous data concerning air pressure on curved surfaces must be inaccurate. They built their own wind tunnel and over 200 model wings in order to make their own pressure tables. Their tables became the first reliable ones ever made.

In 1902 they tried a third glider, using their new information. It vastly exceeded the success of all previous gliders, with some glides exceeding 600 feet (180 meters). This led the brothers to plan and build a power airplane. In 1903, at a cost just under one thousand dollars, the plane was complete. Its wings measured 40.5 feet (12 meters), and it weighed 750 pounds (340 kilograms) with the pilot. In September of 1903, they arrived in Kittyhawk, but a series of bad storms and defects delayed them. However, on December 17, 1903, they achieved flight.

Over the next few years, their experiments produced even longer and better flights. On October 5, 1905, their plane flew for 24.2 miles (38.9 kilometers) in just over 38 minutes. In 1908, they closed a contract with the United States Department of War for the first military airplane ever made.

The brothers went on to exhibit flight in France and the United States as well as to teach others to be pilots. Eventually, the inevitable happened: on September 17, 1908, Orville and his passenger, Lieutenant Thomas E. Selfridge, crashed due to a malfunction. Orville recovered but Selfridge died. However, the work of the brothers continued until Wilbur died of typhoid fever in 1912. Orville carried on alone until his death in 1948. Today they are remembered as the fathers of modern flight.

Suggested Activity

Models Construct model airplanes from paper, testing their aerodynamic qualities. Conduct experiments and use your data to build the best possible plane. An excellent resource is Teacher Created Materials #281 *Thematic Unit: Flight.*

'Teens Overview

- World War I began as a local war between Austria-Hungary and Serbia. As a result of conflicts in the Balkan states, the rise of nationalism, and a series of international alliances, it rapidly became a general European struggle. Eventually it became a global war involving 32 nations. The 28 nations known as the *Allies and Associated Powers* included Great Britain, France, Russia, Italy, and, eventually, the United States. The *Central Powers* consisted of Germany, Austria-Hungary, Turkey, and Bulgaria. Acts of heroism and tragedy filled the newspapers daily, and people on the home fronts focussed their energies to "helping the cause" in whatever ways they could.

- Heroes and villains came to the forefront throughout the war and in its aftermath. Frequently mentioned names included Lenin, Rasputin, Mussolini, Lloyd George, Kitchener, Von Hindenburg, Mata Hari, the Kaiser, Tsar Nicholas II, Trotsky, Stalin, the Red Baron, General John J. Pershing, Bernard Baruch, and Herbert Hoover.

- Trenches, tanks, submarines, zeppelins, poison gas, long-range bombers, and fighter planes were used for the first time.

- Power in Europe and Russia shifted dramatically both during the Great War and as a result of its effects. New leaders offered hope to the impoverished and battle-scarred masses.

- Labor disputes continued. A tragic fire at the Triangle Shirtwaist Company killed 146 employees. That and other tragedies built momentum for enhanced labor laws.

- The call for women's rights, especially the vote, grew as the economy at home depended more and more on the work of women while the men were away fighting the war. The end of the decade brought victory to the suffragists.

- President Woodrow Wilson's Fourteen Point plan for peace included the formation of a League of Nations.

- Mexico faced a revolution in an effort to oust its dictator, Porfirio Diaz.

- Inventor Thomas Edison developed talking pictures, which would soon revolutionize the entertainment industry. In Hollywood, California, a film mecca was begun by Cecil B. De Mille. A small group of actors began a new company, United Artists, in order to produce films.

- The Indianapolis Motor Speedway held its first five hundred mile race. The first winner, Ray Harroun, drove at the speed of seventy-five miles per hour.

- In 1913 the Sixteenth Amendment to the U.S. Constitution made income taxes legal. Three months later the Seventeenth Amendment was ratified. It provided for the election of United States senators by direct, popular vote. Prior to this, they had been elected by their state legislatures.

- The Selective Service began its draft of young men for military duty.

- China saw its last emperor and closed the 260-year reign of the Manchu dynasty.

- The new luxury liner, the *Titanic*, struck an iceberg on its maiden voyage and sunk. Nearly 1,600 people drowned due to a shortage of lifeboats on board.

- New Mexico and Arizona joined the United States in 1912.

- Jim Thorpe, a Native American, amazed audiences at the 1912 Olympics. Many considered him the greatest athlete ever. However, he was later stripped of his medals for having played professional baseball for a short period of time.

- The Panama Canal, once considered an impossible venture, was opened in 1913.

- Kindergartens became popular in the United States, and several states added them to their school programs.

- Daylight savings time began in an effort to save electricity to help the war effort.

The Great War

Fought on three continents, the war that lasted from 1914 through 1918 was known simply as the Great War. When a second such war began, its name was then changed to World War I. Below are listed some of the major events of the war that tore nations—and the world—apart.

1911   Germany is growing in power, and the French and the British are alarmed. The Germans send a gunboat to Agadir, Morocco, which is under French protection, resulting in the Agadir Crisis in which France and Germany narrowly avoid a war. France and Great Britain feel certain that Germany is a threat to world peace. Austria-Hungary and Britain increase their respective navies.

Turkish rule over the Balkan states is showing breakdown. Revolt seems certain.

1912   The Balkan states revolt against Turkey.

1913   Having defeated the Turks, the Balkan states begin to fight among themselves. Other nations take sides in their war.

1914   Archduke Francis Ferdinand, heir to the throne of Austria-Hungary, and his wife, Sophie, are assassinated on June 28 while visiting Sarajevo, Bosnia, part of the Austro-Hungarian Empire. The assassin, Gavrilo Princip, is a Serbian. Austria-Hungary blames the Serbians and declares war on them and on Russia, which is fighting in defense of Serbia. Germany joins forces with Austria-Hungary, as does Turkey. The three are the Central Powers. Germans march through Belgium and attempt to take Paris. Belgium joins forces with Serbia, as does Britain which has a treaty with Belgium. Russia, Serbia, France, Belgium, and Britain become the Allies. Germany's Kaiser calls for victory by autumn. The Allies are confident the war will end by Christmas.

Trench warfare is used for the first time in Belgium and France. The Allies halt the Germans at the bloody Battle of the Marne, protecting Paris for the time being. The Russian General Samsonov shoots himself after failing to invade Germany and losing 120,000 men to Germany as prisoners.

On Christmas Day in Ypres, Belgium, soldiers from both sides gather together peacefully talking and sharing cigarettes. By the end of the year, there are hundreds of thousands of casualties.

1915   Germany uses chlorine gas in Ypres, the first time poison gas has been used in war. The Germans wear face masks to protect themselves.

Russia attempts to keep Germany out of Poland. Bulgaria aids Germany, and they overtake Poland, capturing Serbia. The Allies fight to protect the Dardanelles Channel, which is a crucial passageway for the Russians. It is blocked by Turkey. They make several attempts from the Gallipoli Peninsula, but they repeatedly fail and finally withdraw. The Anzacs (Australian and New Zealand Army Corps), who have just joined the war, are particularly noted for their bravery at Gallipoli.

The Great War (cont.)

1915 *(cont.)*

A British nurse named Edith Cavell, head of the Brussels School of Nursing, is executed by the Germans for helping British soldiers to escape.

The British liner, the *Lusitania*, the largest passenger ship in the world, is torpedoed by a German U-boat (submarine) off the Irish coast. The ship is unarmed and carries nearly 2,000 passengers and crew members, many of whom die, including nearly 130 Americans. The Germans have orders to stop all supplies from reaching Britain; every ship is suspect. The United States is outraged, and many believe that President Wilson will not be able to keep the United States out of the war, although Germany apologizes for its error.

Italy joins the Allies.

1916

The Battle of Jutland, the only major navy battle of the war, is fought and hundreds die. There is no victor.

France experiences massive casualties at Verdun where Germans use flame throwers and gas shells. Meanwhile, the Allies attack at the Somme, attempting to relieve the soldiers at Verdun. However, nearly two million die.

Lord Kitchener, the British secretary of war, is drowned when his ship hits a mine. Kitchener is famous for his recruiting poster. David Lloyd George replaces Kitchener.

In September, the Allies introduce their new weapon, the tank.

Russia attacks Austria, gaining sixty miles (100 kilometers) and 400,000 prisoners.

President Wilson is reelected under the slogan "He kept us out of the war."

1917

The Russian people, tired of the war, begin to revolt. They blame the tsar for their two million casualties and impoverished conditions at home. V. I. Lenin and the Bolsheviks overtake the government and sign an armistice with Germany. Russia is out of the war.

In April, after three years of attempting to stay out of the war and bring peace to the world, President Wilson and the United States Congress declare war on the Germans. Public opinion is almost completely won over due to an intercepted telegram from the German foreign minister to his ambassador in Mexico. In it, the Germans offer to aid Mexico in recovering its previous holdings, now a part of the United States (Texas, New Mexico, and Arizona). Millions of Americans enlist in the U.S. Army and travel "Over There" to the Western front.

The Italians experience total defeat at Caporetto, where the Germans and Austria-Hungary gain huge areas of land. The surviving Italian soldiers retreat, leaving their weapons behind on the battlefield.

China declares war on Germany and Austria.

Germany creates the Hindenburg Line, a 31-mile (50 kilometer) system of trenches with concrete dugouts, barbed wire, and access to railroads for supplies.

Passchendaele, France, becomes the scene of one of the bloodiest battles in the war. It is fought in constant rain and mud, and the shooting is relentless.

The Red Cross receives the Nobel peace prize for its volunteer work on the battlefields of the world.

The Great War (cont.)

1918   President Wilson outlines Fourteen Points for peace, including the formation of a League of Nations to protect independence for all nations.

In the Spring, the Germans leave the Hindenburg Line to make two offensives. The first is at the Marne, where the Allies once again defend themselves with heavy casualties. At the same time, they battle the other offensive at the Lys River in Belgium. The German general Erich von Ludendorff asks the Kaiser to make peace. Ludendorff is dismissed from his duties.

Thousands of American troops arrive in France. A series of Allied counterattacks result in victories. An Allied war victory seems imminent.

The ace German pilot, the Red Baron, is killed. Allies pay tribute to him and his skill, although he was an enemy.

Hundreds of Germans surrender in the face of intense attacks by Allied planes and tanks.

Turkey is defeated by the British, led by General Edmund Allenby. Lt. Col. T. E. Lawrence has been highly effective in the war against the Turks.

Austria-Hungary becomes a republic and is out of the war.

An epidemic of influenza strikes around the world, causing millions of deaths.

Nicholas, the former tsar of Russia, and his family are executed by the Bolsheviks.

At 11 A.M. on the eleventh day of the eleventh month, an armistice is signed by the Allies and Germany. The four-year war is over. France and Belgium have been nearly destroyed.

The United States comes out of the war with its land intact and its economy strong. It is in a favorable position to become a major world leader. Many European nations are devastated and impoverished.

1919   Terms for peace are agreed upon by the victorious nations at the Palace of Versailles in Paris, France. President Wilson urges the creation of a League of Nations. The German chancellor resigns, refusing to sign the treaty. It calls for Germany to pay 33 million dollars to the Allies in reparations and to reduce its army and arsenal of weapons. On June 28, two German representatives silently enter the Palace and sign the treaty, and still silent, they leave. Germany feels it has been forced to accept unreasonable terms. Poland, a part of Russia for fifty years, is made an independent country by the treaty.

German prisoners of war sink seventy German ships docked at Scapa Flow, Scotland. They say they are under orders never to surrender their warships.

There is a Communist revolt in Germany, but it is squelched.

The Fascist Party is formed by Benito Mussolini in Italy and grows rapidly.

Suggested Activities

Research Have each student research one major event of World War I and present the information he or she finds to the class.

Cartography Draw maps showing European boundaries before World War I and after. Also draw a map of modern-day Europe.

Read and Write Collect firsthand accounts of the war and share them in the class as a reader's theater. Then have the students write their own accounts as though they are soldiers fighting the war or civilians caught in the middle of it.

The Unsinkable Titanic

In April of 1912, approximately 2,200 passengers and crew members boarded the *Titanic*, a new luxury liner ready for its maiden voyage. The *Titanic* had the best of everything, and only the elite could afford passage. Some even paid more than $4,000 for the trip, while many of the crew did not even earn $1,000 in a year. The ship's promoters claimed that their vessel was unsinkable, primarily because its hull had sixteen watertight compartments. Even if two compartments flooded, the ship would still float. Everyone had complete confidence in the boat.

A number of famous people were on board, including millionaire John Jacob Astor and his wife, as well as Isidor and Ida Straus, the wealthy department store owners. In general, the passengers had complete confidence in the ship because the best design and latest technology was at their fingertips.

Late on the night of April 14, the *Titanic* was sailing in the North Atlantic Ocean on its trip from Southampton, England, to New York City. The ship was traveling at a speed of twenty-one knots (nautical miles per hour), which was nearly top speed. Since there was danger of icebergs in the area, the ship's speed was far too fast. At 11:40 P.M., the *Titanic* rubbed alongside an iceberg for approximately ten seconds. That was enough. The hull of the ship was made of a type of steel that became brittle in the icy waters of the North Atlantic. Several small cracks appeared instantly, and seams unriveted. Water started to pour inside, weakening the hull still further.

Six distress signals were sent out immediately. Another passenger ship, the *California*, was just twenty minutes away at the time; however, its radio operator was not on duty, so no one there heard the *Titanic's* signal. Another ship, the *Carpathia*, was approximately four hours away, and it responded to the signal. However, when the *Carpathia* arrived at 4:00 A.M., it was too late for many of the passengers. The *Titanic* had long since sunk. Just after 2:00 A.M., water had flooded through the hull to the ship's bow, causing the entire vessel to split in two.

At first, the passengers aboard the ship were calm, expecting to reach lifeboats with ease and then be rescued by other ships. They did not know that the *Titanic's* lifeboats only had room for approximately 1,200 people, far less than the number of people on board. When the passengers and crew saw how dire the situation was, many stepped aside for younger passengers to board lifeboats safely. Among these heroes were the Astors and Strauses. Captain Edward J. Smith went down with his ship. In all, 705 people survived the wreck, most of them women and children. The remaining 1,517 died in the icy waters of the North Atlantic Ocean.

When the ship was first endangered, the band on board began to play a ragtime melody to encourage the passengers. As time passed and the situation grew grim, they continued to play, but this time it was an old English hymn calling for mercy and compassion from God.

In 1985, a team of scientists found the wreckage of the *Titanic* 12,500 feet (3,800 meters) beneath the sea. Although people had previously thought that a large gash was immediately ripped in the boat because of the iceberg, the scientists were able to prove that the steel composition of the hull was truly the fatal flaw as was the speed at which the boat was traveling.

Suggested Activities

Read Find reports of the studies made from the 1985 expedition. What did they reveal about the ship and its passengers? What did the scientists do to find the wreck?

Writing Imagine you are a *Titanic* survivor, floating away on a lifeboat while hundreds of others are struggling in the freezing water. Write what you think and experience.

Jim Thorpe

Jim Thorpe is widely considered one of the greatest athletes of all time. His talents ranged from football to baseball to track and field, and he was successful in all those areas. Born in Oklahoma in 1887, Thorpe, a Native American, began to show his athletic skill at the Carlisle Indian Industrial School in Pennsylvania. Because of him, the small school achieved national recognition.

In the 1912 Olympics in Stockholm, Sweden, Thorpe became the first athlete to win both the pentathlon and decathlon. He also came in first in the 200-meter dash and the 1,500-meter run. Russia's Tsar Nicholas II sent Thorpe a silver model of a Viking ship as a tribute to his skill, and the King of Sweden called him "the greatest athlete in the world." Thorpe had earned a small salary as a baseball player in 1909 and 1910 and because this gave him professional status, not the amateur status required to compete in Olympic games, his medals were taken away about a month after he received them. In 1982, twenty-nine years after Thorpe's death, the International Olympic Committee reconsidered and restored the medals.

A multitalented athlete, Jim Thorpe played professional baseball for three major league teams (1913–1919) and football for seven teams (1915–1930). He became the first president of the American Professional Football Association (now the National Football League) and one of the first men admitted into the National Football Foundation's Hall of Fame (1951). Today, though athletes show masterful skill in their fields, it is quite rare for a single athlete to compete so successfully in several different sports.

Suggested Activities

Pentathlon As a tribute to Thorpe, and as a means to show your own athletic skill, hold your own classroom pentathlon. The traditional events are the long jump, javelin throw, 200-meter run, discus throw, and 1,500-meter run. However these events are not conducive to classes. Choose five activities to hold in your pentathlon. They can be fun like banana tossing or hopscotch. Most importantly, have fun!

Olympics The Olympic Games of 1912 were also notable for two other reasons. First, they were the first Olympics that allowed women to compete, although they only did so in swimming and diving. Find out more about these groundbreaking women athletes of the 1912 games. The second reason is that the Americans won thirteen out of the twenty-eight possible golds. Who were the gold medal winners of the 1912 Olympics?

Multitalented Athletes Some athletes have played professionally in more than one sport, including Bo Jackson and Michael Jordan. Name any other athletes you can who have done this and tell the sports in which they have played. Have any of them been as successful in two or more sports as Jim Thorpe was?

Panama Canal

For many years, sailors had wished for a shortened way to navigate their ships from the Pacific Ocean to the Atlantic. At the turn of the century, the journey took seven thousand miles (11,270 kilometers). However, beginning on August 15, 1914, it became a trip of forty miles (64.4 kilometers).

Panama is a small nation lying at the base of Central America and at the northwest corner of Columbia, South America. Its area is relatively narrow. In the 1880s, the French attempted to build a canal across the nation, but their plans were ineffective. They also had to deal with rampant jungle diseases such as malaria and yellow fever. France gave up its efforts.

In 1904, the United States, under the leadership of President Theodore Roosevelt, gained the rights to build a canal through Panama. The project began with a vengeance. Americans arrived in Central America by the thousands, hoping to capitalize on high wages. However, the problems of disease and climate were the same for the Americans as they had been for the French. In order to succeed, different tactics had to be taken.

President Roosevelt hired a chief engineer, General George W. Goethals, to head the project. Goethals and his team developed a system of locks that would raise and lower the water level for the passage of ships. General William Gorgas was brought on board to curb the effects of malaria and yellow fever. Although he was not able to stop the diseases, he did reduce the death toll from thirty-nine per thousand workers in 1906 to seven per thousand workers by 1914. However, throughout the project, nearly six thousand workers died.

The entire project required the removal of 240 million cubic yards of earth. The number of workers employed reached, at its peak, 40,000, and the cost for the project, which took ten years to complete, was more than $350 million.

Finally complete in summer 1914, the Panama Canal let pass its first ship, the *Alcon*, on August 15 with a shipload of officials on board. As they sailed the meager miles from ocean to ocean, no one seemed to mind the toll the canal had taken, and they rejoiced in the fifteen or so hours it took to sail completely through the passage. Although the canal could never repay the lives lost, it has more than repaid the financial costs. Today, approximately seventy ships pass through the canal each day at a cost of approximately $7,000 in tolls.

Suggested Activities

Cartography Draw Panama and the location of the canal on a map. Also draw a map showing the route that needed to be taken by ships prior to the canal's completion in 1914.

Disease Find out about malaria and yellow fever and how they were treated in the years of the Panama Canal's construction. Also find out how they are treated today.

Research and Discussion Find out the importance to the United States of the Panama Canal. Determine why it was considered worth losing lives and spending money in order to construct the canal. Discuss what you find.

History Trace the history of the canal from the time it was built until the present. Does the United States still maintain rights to the canal?

Twenties Overview

When Warren Harding campaigned for the presidency in 1920, he promised a "return to normalcy." For most Americans, this meant a return to life as it had been before World War I, but the war had changed America and the world too much. Harding's brief administration is remembered for its corruption, especially the Teapot Dome scandal. After Harding's untimely death in 1923, Calvin Coolidge was sworn into office. Believing that "The chief business of America is business," Coolidge shepherded tax laws through Congress that were mostly favorable to businesses. In 1928 Herbert Hoover, who promised "four years of prosperity," won the presidency by a landslide. After the stock market crash of 1929, Hoover was largely blamed for the disaster.

Prohibition became the law of the land in 1920. No one is certain whether drinking increased during Prohibition or not, but it did spread among women and youth and became a symbol of defiance. It also gave rise to organized crime and increased violence. Bootlegging was a big business.

By the end of the twenties many families had automobiles—a novelty at the beginning of the decade. Radios brought nightly comedy shows and news to families throughout the country and changed political campaigns. People flocked to the movies, and in 1927 movies had sound.

Musicians George Gershwin and Aaron Copland, writers Ernest Hemingway and F. Scott Fitzgerald, and artists Mary Cassatt and Grant Wood became prominent. In the predominantly black-populated section of Harlem in New York City, the Harlem Renaissance produced a host of great African American writers, artists, and musicians.

Fostered by presidents who favored business, the stock market reached new heights before the crash on October 29, 1929. At first President Hoover believed that the situation was temporary and refused to allow government aid for homeless and out-of-work people. His seeming insensitivity to the plight of the American people cost him the election of 1930.

For Discussion

1. What innovations were making their way into the everyday lives of the American people during the 1920s? How did these innovations change the lifestyles of the typical American?

2. Can you imagine your life now with only radio and no television? How would your life be different if that were the case?

3. Was it fair for the American public to blame Hoover for the effects of the stock market crash? How could this disaster possibly have been avoided?

4. What safety improvements have been made in the automobile since its invention? What problems has the automobile brought to our lives? How would your life be different without the automobile?

Black Tuesday

On Tuesday, October 29, 1929, the stock market collapsed. Ten billion dollars in stock were lost in very heavy trading in only a few hours that day. Stocks that had sold for twenty to forty dollars a share just a few weeks ago now sold for pennies. High rollers who had been speculating in the market were immediately bankrupted. President Hoover's claim that the country's business was "on a sound and prosperous basis" proved to be tragically incorrect. In the weeks and months that followed, the effects were even more profound. Five thousand banks failed and closed their doors, causing over nine million people to lose their savings accounts. For the first three years following the stock market crash, an average of 100,000 jobs were lost each week. Since so many people were out of work or in danger of losing their jobs, people began to economize and avoided unnecessary purchases. As demand for goods decreased, businesses were forced to lay off workers, adding to unemployment. Soon, people's money ran out, and they were unable to pay their mortgages and other debts. They lost their homes, cars, and other valuables. Hardship became a way of life. Some families were forced to live in shacks made of discarded lumber and cardboard. These shanty towns became known as "Hoovervilles," and the newspapers they used for blankets were called "Hoover blankets."

Suggested Activities

Cause and Effect Briefly review with the class the relationship between cause and effect. Establish that cause is the reason something happens and effect is the action that takes place in response to the cause. Discuss with the class some of the following causes and effects from the paragraphs about Black Tuesday.

a. People economized and avoided unnecessary purchases (cause); demand for goods decreased and businesses laid off additional workers (effects).

b. The stock market crashed (cause); high rollers were bankrupted, banks failed, and nine million people lost their savings (effects).

c. Millions of people were out of work (cause); they began to economize (effect).

Priorities Group the students and have them make a list of at least 15 ways they think families during the depression began to economize. In whole-group compare the different lists. Extend the activity with a discussion of how they would economize today if their family support member suddenly lost his or her job. Compare these methods with the lists for depression families.

Simulated Crash To help students understand how and why the stock market crashed, engage them in a simulation activity. Complete directions and game cards can be found on pages 85 to 88 in Teacher Created Materials #480—*American History Simulations*.

Prohibition

What is Prohibition? Prohibition, or the outlawing of the consumption of all alcoholic beverages, may seem like an unmanageable task on a national level. At the beginning of the twentieth century, there were those who thought otherwise. At the outset, the majority of Americans supported the Eighteenth Amendment, believing that a world without liquor would be a better place. After a few years, it became apparent that its drawbacks outweighed any possible benefits.

Alcohol-Related Problems Alcoholism was a prevalent problem in nineteenth century America. Men would drink away whole paychecks, leaving no money to support their families. Some women's groups, religious groups, and reformers fought for prohibition. Many states became dry; that is, they passed laws which made it illegal to buy or to sell liquor. The fight did not stop there, however, because some people wanted to make the entire nation dry. This would take a constitutional amendment.

Why Prohibition Was Supported Prohibition was supported by religious groups that believed drinking was sinful. Business leaders also favored prohibition, thinking it would reduce absenteeism at work. Other groups blamed poverty, disease, and crime on alcoholism. Physicians spoke out about the dangers of alcohol consumption to unborn babies and noted that in large families where the parents drank, the children were often mentally retarded. When the United States entered World War I, a strong argument for personal sacrifice and the need for grain to aid in the war effort led Congress to pass the Eighteenth Amendment. It read: "After one year from the ratification of this article the manufacture, sale, or transportation of intoxicating liquors within, the importation thereof into, or the exportation thereof from the United States and all territory subject to the jurisdiction thereof for beverage purposes is hereby prohibited." Ratified by 36 states in January of 1919, the Prohibition Amendment took effect in January 1920.

Why Prohibition Did Not Work Prohibition made drinking more attractive to many people. Consumption of alcohol by women and young people increased. Gangsters like Al Capone of Chicago took over the illegal activity of selling liquor. Speakeasies popped up all over the country — by 1933 there were more than 200,000 speakeasies throughout the United States. Prohibition laws became the most disliked and disobeyed laws in U.S. history. Congress did not foresee problems with enforcement of the law and did not provide enough money for agents.

Effects of Prohibition The restrictions of Prohibition probably caused the outrageous behaviors of the 1920s. Speakeasies, nightclubs, and blind pigs had abundant business. Making "bathtub gin" and brewing beer became popular pastimes. Disregard for Prohibition created contempt for other laws and made crime a big business.

Suggested Activities

Class Debate Have two groups of students prepare for and debate this question: Could the lessons of Prohibition be applied to the current drug problem in the United States?

Response Ask students to respond in writing to this question: Should Prohibition be reinstated? Why or why not? Discuss their written responses in whole group.

Words Have the students define these and other Prohibition-era terms: *dry, bootleggers, rumrunners, temperance, speakeasies, teetotaler, jake leg, blind pig.*

Campaign Many communities and large corporations have created campaign slogans, signs, and materials against drinking and driving. Assign individuals or pairs to create a poster that might help convince people not to drink and drive. Display all the posters on the classroom walls.

Coming to America

Immigration was not new to the 1920s, but the complexion for the situation changed dramatically in the early part of the twentieth century. From its earliest years the United States of America had an open door policy toward immigrants, placing few restrictions on the number of people entering this country. It was not until 1882 that the first law was passed banning people from a specific country. The Chinese Exclusion Act forbade Chinese laborers because it was feared that they would work for lower pay. In 1907 a "gentleman's agreement" between the United States and Japan barred Japanese immigrants.

In the early 1900s there were two groups who sought to have the doors closed to certain ethnic members. American laborers feared that they would lose their jobs to new immigrants, who were willing to work for lower wages. A second group believed that the newcomers were inferior. Still, it was not until 1917 that restrictions were in place, preventing thirty-three different categories of people from obtaining entry to the United States.

Immigration in the 1920s changed in another important way. Prior to 1880 newcomers originated mostly from countries in northern and western Europe. When the immigrant population shifted to southern and eastern European countries, some Americans became alarmed at the customs and languages. World War I placed a temporary halt to the problem as very few people came to America during that period. Once the war ended, the wave of immigrants rose steadily, with over 600,000 people arriving in 1921. With the passage of a new law that same year, immigration was limited by a quota system. The National Origins Act of 1924 established severe quotas for southern and eastern European countries. For example, 100,000 Italians had

arrived in one year in the early 1900s, but the new quota limited Italy to 5,082 people per year; Greece was allowed only 307 people per year, while Russia was permitted 2,784 per year. Not until the 1960s, when Lyndon Johnson became president, did those quota laws change.

Suggested Activities

Respond Have the students respond to this question: Are quota laws for immigration fair or necessary? With the class, discuss some possible solutions for this dilemma.

Charts Divide the students into groups and have them make charts comparing 1920s immigration with current immigration. Include topics such as length of travel, mode of travel, cities of entry, and countries of origin.

References

Do People Grow on Family Trees? by Ira Wolfman (Workman Publishing, 1991).
Teacher Created Materials #234 *Thematic Unit—Immigration.*

Transatlantic Flight

After World War I, the availability of surplus equipment and trained pilots led to the growth of commercial aviation. Barnstormers presented air shows and provided short rides for the public, and airplanes carried mail across the country. Soon attention focused on the possibility of transatlantic flight. In 1919 a wealthy hotel man offered a $25,000 prize to anyone who could fly nonstop from New York to Paris.

Charles Lindbergh

Such a flight was extremely hazardous. The pilot would have to fly thousands of miles over a stormy ocean and would face rain clouds, dense fog, and even icebergs. Over the next eight years several pilots, including explorer Richard Evelyn Byrd, tried and failed. Then, in May of 1927, an unknown airmail pilot named Charles Lindbergh accepted the challenge.

His plane, the *Spirit of St. Louis*, was ill equipped for such a dangerous undertaking. It had no radio, and the pilot's seat was a wicker chair. Because the plane carried as much fuel as possible, there was no room left for any excess weight. All that Lindbergh carried on board with him was a quart of water, a paper sack full of sandwiches, a map, letters of introduction, and a rubber raft. Staying awake and alert throughout the 33½ hour flight proved to be a major challenge for Lindbergh.

A raucous, cheering crowd greeted Lindbergh when he landed in Paris. After meeting European kings and princes, Lindbergh and the *Spirit of St. Louis* returned home, where he was showered with parades and celebrations. A world hero at the age of 25, Lindbergh's feat inspired a popular song, a dance, and popular fashions.

Lindbergh refused numerous offers for moneymaking opportunities following his historic flight. He continued to be a strong advocate of aviation and flew 50 combat missions in World War II. In 1953 he earned a Pulitzer prize for *The Spirit of St. Louis*, which chronicled his historic flight.

Suggested Activities

Aviation History Teach students about the history of flight. Read aloud the book *The Wright Brothers: How They Invented the Airplane* by Russell Freedman (Holiday House, 1991). Discuss the adversities Lindbergh faced.

Female Pilot In 1922 Bessie Coleman became the first licensed African American pilot in America. Because of the existing prejudice against blacks, Coleman had to travel to France, where she learned how to fly. Coleman was honored in 1995 by the U.S. Post Office with a 32-cent stamp. Have students research this woman's background and accomplishments.

Earhart Amelia Earhart became as famous as Lindbergh when she flew solo across the Atlantic in 1932. In 1937 she attempted to fly around the world. Her plane disappeared somewhere in the South Pacific six weeks into the journey. Assign students to research what happened to Earhart and her co-pilot.

Mapping Assign students to create a map of Lindbergh's flight across the Atlantic.

References
Lindbergh by Chris L. Demarest (Crown Publishers, Inc., 1993).
Barnstormers & Daredevils by K. C. Tessendorf (Macmillan, 1988).

Thirties Overview

The stock market crash of 1929 brought an abrupt end to the good times that had preceded it. As the days wore on, it became evident that the economy was not going to be able to mend itself. President Hoover firmly believed that the government should stay out of business and refused to offer any help until 1932. Billions of dollars were lent to failing businesses under the Reconstruction Finance Corporation bill. It was too little and far too late to help end the epidemic of bank failures. As for the unemployed, Hoover felt that any type of assistance would produce even more out-of-work people. His advice to the needy was to seek help from charitable organizations, but they, too, were overburdened and lacked sufficient donations. Most people felt that their president had forsaken them and was indifferent to their plight.

In the election of 1932, Herbert Hoover was soundly defeated by Franklin Delano Roosevelt, who promised the nation a New Deal. One of the first things the new president did was to close all banks so that federal auditors could examine their records. Only then were financially sound banks reopened. Next on his list was getting people back to work. On March 31, 1933, the Civilian Conservation Corps provided jobs for nearly three million young men. More helpful legislation quickly followed. In fact, Roosevelt's first one hundred days in office produced a flurry of legislation that would help the economy recover.

Recovery was a long, slow process, however, and millions suffered from homelessness and unemployment. In the Midwest, erosion problems and drought caused a dust storm that wiped out farms from Oklahoma to Texas. Thousands of "Okies" migrated to California's fertile land in search of work. What they faced was not enough jobs and prejudice from the Californians. Throughout the country, factory and mill workers began to stage strikes for better pay and working conditions. Tactics such as sit-in strikes enabled workers to gain decent benefits and safe conditions.

Radio dominated American life, much like television would decades later. Through his fireside chats, President Roosevelt explained his policies and reassured America. Programs such as *The Lone Ranger* and *Amos' 'n' Andy* helped people forget their troubles. At the movies, Bugs Bunny and Porky Pig debuted and kept everyone laughing. Double features, two movies for the price of one, helped people economize on entertainment. Child star Shirley Temple charmed audiences with her singing and dancing. Even President Roosevelt acknowledged the tiny actor's contributions.

At the end of the 1930s, focus shifted overseas with the rise of fascism in Germany, Italy, and Japan. At first, Roosevelt did not challenge the isolationists, but after war began in 1939, the nation rallied firmly behind Great Britain and its allies. America was quickly swept into a world war and a new era in history.

About the Great Depression

This overview will help students understand more about the causes and effects of the Great Depression. Use it as a study guide and a springboard for discussions.

Definition The Great Depression was a period of severe decline in business activity accompanied by falling prices and high unemployment. During the Depression nearly 13 million people were out of work, banks closed, savings were wiped out, and the stock market collapsed.

Causes A number of factors worked together to cause the Great Depression. Six of them are listed here.

1. Businesses during the twenties had kept prices and profits high while keeping wages low. This meant that labor could not afford to buy what it produced.

2. After World War I farmers kept up their high levels of production, and surpluses piled up. Supply became greater than demand, thus driving prices down.

3. Industry had built more and larger plants, allowing them to produce more goods than they could sell.

4. The introduction of labor-saving machinery put men out of jobs in a number of industries.

5. World War I left the worldwide economy shaky.

6. Installment buying allowed people to purchase on credit, and people piled up debts. They used their money to buy stocks on margin, hoping that prices would rise and they would make a profit.

Effects The effects of the Great Depression were many and included the obvious—hunger, poverty, and homelessness. Another effect was psychological in nature. Men were expected to work, and joblessness was considered a result of laziness. When millions could not find jobs during the Depression, they felt ashamed, even though the situation was not their fault. Some put up a brave, false front, while others kept to themselves to avoid revealing their situation and true feelings.

How People Coped People were forced to change their lives during the Depression. There was no unemployment insurance to fall back on or Social Security benefits, either. People found ways to cope the best they could. Belt tightening became a way of life. Some people had to turn to charity, friends, or family for help. Two or more families often crowded into one apartment, splitting the rent. Meat became a luxury, as did eating out at a restaurant. When electric bills were too high for some to pay, they resorted to kerosene lamps.

Government Intervention As the Depression raged on, it was obvious that some government help would be necessary to get the economy back on its feet. President Hoover did not believe in either government intervention in business or direct assistance for the people. When Franklin Roosevelt was elected president, he quickly took action. In a flurry of legislative activity during a period known as the First Hundred Days, Congress passed a number of innovative laws, some of which are still in effect today.

"First Lady of the World"

She was a person of action, a friend of the poor and oppressed, and a champion of human rights. Her actions helped change the role of first lady, and she became one of the most beloved figures in U.S. history. Her name was Anna Eleanor Roosevelt.

Eleanor Roosevelt

Born to Anna and Elliott Roosevelt on October 11, 1884, she lived a privileged life, complete with servants, governesses, and maids to attend her and her two brothers. Despite the family's wealth, however, Roosevelt's childhood was an unhappy one. Her mother, a beauty and a member of New York's wealthy society, cruelly nicknamed her daughter "granny," which made Roosevelt feel that she was ugly and awkward. Before she was ten years old, her parents and a brother died. She lived with her grandmother and, at fifteen, was sent to boarding school in England.

Here she was introduced to new ideas which helped draw her out of her shell. After returning to the U.S. in 1902, she caught the eye of her handsome, distant cousin, Franklin Delano Roosevelt, and the two married on March 17, 1905.

The young couple quickly became a family. They had four children in their first five years together, and two more children followed. Like other wealthy young wives, Eleanor Roosevelt served on charity boards and attended classes in literature, art, and music. When Roosevelt's political career took off, she became a politician's wife, speaking on behalf of her husband, doing volunteer work, and visiting the troops during World War I. In 1918, she discovered some love notes from Lucy Mercer to Roosevelt. Devastated, she poured herself into social causes—world peace, civil rights, and women's issues. The marriage remained intact, but it was never the same for the deeply wounded Eleanor Roosevelt.

In the summer of 1921, Franklin Roosevelt contracted poliomyeltis. Seven years later, with his wife's support, he reentered politics. His legs were paralyzed but not his mind. She became his eyes and legs, visiting places that he could not. Unlike other presidents' wives, she did not stay in the background but began campaigning for a variety of social issues. Even after Franklin Roosevelt's death, Eleanor Roosevelt continued her work as a spokesperson for human decency.

Suggested Activities

The United Nations Find out about Eleanor Roosevelt's role in the United Nations. Explain what the Universal Declaration of Human Rights is and how it is enforced.

Women's Rights Eleanor Roosevelt began a series of regular press conferences for women only, and she supported the idea that women had a right to work. Make a list of some of her other views about women's rights.

Civil Rights Mrs. Roosevelt invited African American singer Marian Anderson to perform at the Washington Monument. Find out what events led to this performance and Roosevelt's role in them.

Olympic Star

The tenth child born to Henry and Emma Owens was sickly as a child. His lungs were weak and remained that way even into adulthood, but James Cleveland "Jesse" Owens was a fighter, and someday he would make a name for himself.

J. C., as he was commonly known, was born on September 12, 1913. His parents were sharecroppers, and his mother did other people's laundry to earn extra money. There was little time for school for J. C. and his siblings because they had to work in the cotton fields. In 1921 Henry Owens sold his mule and moved his family to Cleveland, Ohio, in search of a better life. Although he could not find steady employment, the children could attend school. When a teacher asked the shy J. C. his name, she heard him say "Jesse" rather than J.C. From then on he was Jesse Owens.

Jesse Owens

When he was only 14 Coach Charles Riley took an interest in Owens and helped him train. Owens began breaking national records while he was still in high school. When Ohio State University recruited Owens for their track team, he did not think he could afford it. Coach Riley found Owens work operating a freight elevator and also got a job for Henry Owens as a janitor. During a meet on May 25, 1935, Owens broke five world records and tied another. The following year he went to the Olympics in Berlin, Germany. Of the 66 participants on the American track and field team, 10, including Owens, were blacks. At that time, Adolf Hitler was in command of Germany. He and his followers believed that the Germans were superior to all other races. Hitler was in attendance at the games as Jesse Owens proved him wrong. First Owens won the 100 meter dash, then the 200 meter dash. After a shaky start in the broad jump he went on to set a record that would stand until 1960. Owens's fourth gold medal at the Olympics came as a member of the relay team.

In 1935 Owens married his high school sweetheart, Ruth, and they had three daughters. At first after the Olympics, Owens was treated like a star. Some people made him business offers, while others tried to take advantage of him. He started his own business with mixed success. Later, he worked with children in a recreation department. On March 31, 1980, Jesse Owens died of lung cancer at the age of 66. He had been greatly honored during his lifetime. President Ford gave him the Medal of Freedom, and President Carter awarded him with the Living Legends Award. Today, Owens' name is synonymous with track and field.

Suggested Activities

Explanations Ask students how experts explain the faster times and longer distances achieved by today's track-and-field stars.

Three D's Owens claimed that the three D's helped make him an Olympic champion: discipline, dedication, and determination. With the students discuss how these three attributes might help a person achieve his/her athletic goals.

Forties Overview

Following World War I, Americans adopted a policy of isolationism. Attention was focused on the Great Depression and events at home, and few people concerned themselves with foreign affairs.

Throughout the twenties and thirties, political and economic unrest brought dictators to power. As the thirties progressed, America modified its previous Neutrality Act, which refused aid to warring nations. To help allies, a "cash and carry" policy allowed the sale of arms to Britain and France. It became apparent soon after Germany's invasion of Poland on September 1, 1939, that America would join the battle. On October 29, 1940, the first peacetime draft was initiated. When Roosevelt ran for his unprecedented third term, war was the major issue. The U.S. did not actively enter the war until the Japanese attack on Pearl Harbor on December 7, 1941. With amazing speed the country mobilized for war.

With the establishment of the WAACs (Women's Auxiliary Army Corps) and WAVES (Women Accepted for Voluntary Emergency Services) in 1942, women began to officially serve in the military. While they were not allowed in actual combat, some served as nurses and others as secretaries. One group of women pilots taught males how to fly and also ferried war planes. As more and more men went off to war, an increasing number of women joined the work force. They took jobs in munitions factories and learned how to build jeeps, tanks, and planes. The government actively recruited more women workers with posters featuring the character Rosie the Riveter. Women were able to earn more money than they ever had, and they found personal satisfaction in knowing they could perform as well as men.

On the home front, every citizen was asked to contribute to the war effort. Sugar, butter, coffee, meat and other foodstuffs were rationed. War ration books were issued in 1942 with coupons for various items. People were encouraged to plant "victory gardens" to help replace rations sent overseas. In addition, a number of other materials were controlled by the government, for example, tin, aluminum, and rubber. War bonds were established by the government to help pay for the war, and even school children were encouraged to buy them.

Roosevelt provided strong leadership for most of World War II. When he died, three months after beginning his fourth term, Vice President Harry Truman took on the role of Commander-in-Chief. On August 15, 1945, the war ended, and America demobilized. The munitions and supplies factories closed. Women in the work force quit or were sent home to make jobs available for the returning veterans. Eager to get on with their lives, the veterans began families. In fact, 63 million babies were born in the U.S. between 1946 and 1960. This increase from the previous birth rate came to be known as the "baby boom." The true impact of this phenomenon would not be felt until the 1960s.

The United Nations

World War I and World War II proved that once major conflict broke out it was nearly impossible for the great powers to remain neutral. Clearly, some type of international organization was needed to maintain lasting peace. The United Nations was founded for this very purpose. Here is an inside look at the United Nations.

History Following World War I, people put their hopes for a lasting peace in the League of Nations, but it was unsuccessful at uniting the various governments of the world. Even the United States did not join the organization despite the fact that its own President Wilson had initiated the idea. Following World War II the Allies created a similar organization and named it the United Nations.

Purpose The main purpose of the United Nations (or UN, as it is called) is to maintain worldwide peace by helping countries resolve their conflicts before they resort to war. Its secondary purposes are to promote equal rights, to develop international cooperation, and to encourage respect for human rights and fundamental freedoms.

Accomplishments Some 350 treaties and conventions have been accepted by the UN members since its inception. World conferences based on special topics have been held. Programs have been established to give early warnings about disasters. Its peace-keeping forces help with disputes among member states.

Membership When it first began on June 6, 1945, fifty one nations signed the charter in San Francisco. Today the United Nations is headquartered in New York City and has grown to include 159 countries or about 98% of the earth's people.

Specialized Agencies Twelve specialized agencies were established by the UN from 1945 to 1959 to organize cooperative help where it is needed. For example, United Nations Children's Emergency Fund *(UNICEF)* provides money, food, and medical supplies in emergency situations. Other agencies include the World Health Organization *(WHO),* and The United Nations Educational, Scientific and Cultural Organization *(UNESCO).*

Suggested Activities

Human Rights The General Assembly of the UN drew up a list of rights that governments should grant to their citizens. Known as the Universal Declaration of Human Rights, it included freedom of speech and religion and the right to education and work. Some countries ignored these rights. Research and find out the role of Amnesty International in preserving these rights.

Debate Conduct a class debate in which students discuss the effectiveness of the UN as a peace-keeping agency.

Diagram Pair the students and have them draw and label a diagram of the United Nations and its governing bodies and related agencies.

UNICEF As a class, participate in the UNICEF fund-raising event at Halloween.

Reference

The United Nations 50th Anniversary Book by Barbara Brenner (Atheneum Books for Young Readers, 1995).

World War II and Its Origins

This list outlines the events which provided the origins of World War II. For an in-depth look at this topic, see the book *The Origins of World War II* by Peter Allen (The Bookwright Press, 1992).

1. At the Paris Peace talks following World War I, Germany was treated harshly. A festering resentment began.

2. President Wilson helped create the League of Nations to prevent future secret alliances among countries. However, the U.S. never joined the League, and both Germany and Japan left the organization.

3. Following the war, the U.S. embraced an isolationist attitude, Great Britain adopted a pacifist foreign policy, and the French pressed for a high level of reparation payments from Germany.

4. When Mussolini became dictator of Italy, he set up the Fascist Party and promoted an aggressive foreign policy. In the Soviet Union, Stalin gained control of the Communist Party and worked to reorganize agriculture and develop industry in his country.

5. At the end of the nineteenth century, Japan had emerged as a world power. In 1931 Japan began a campaign against Manchuria. By 1935 the Japanese had reached the Great Wall of China.

6. When Chiang Kai-shek became dictator of China, he remained on good terms with the U.S. As the leader of the Nationalist Government, he waged civil war against the Communists and initially appeased the Japanese.

7. Throughout the thirties, the Nazi party gained power in Germany, and eventually Hitler was appointed chancellor. After banning all political parties other than the Nazis, he began building his reign of terror and adopted an aggressive expansionist policy.

8. Italian troops invaded Abyssinia and occupied it in May 1936. That same year a small German force marched peacefully into the Rhineland. On July 18, 1936, civil war broke out in Spain.

9. In 1938 Hitler annexed Austria and demanded the Sudetenland, an area of Czechoslovakia with a German population. The Czechoslovakian government resisted but received no support from the Allies, Britain, and France. Britain's prime minister, Neville Chamberlain, chose to appease Hitler in order to avoid war.

10. Late in 1936, Chiang Kai-shek was forced to join the Communists in fighting Japan. By mid-1937 Japan's continued aggression against China caused an unofficial war that lasted throughout World War II. Japan ignored international disapproval and even attacked the U.S. gunboat, *Panay.* Japan apologized for the incident and paid compensation.

11. In 1939 the British policy of appeasement was reversed when German troops invaded Poland. Britain and France, bound by their alliance with Poland, declared war on Germany on September 3.

12. In September of 1940 Japan, Germany, and Italy signed a Tripartite Pact, pledging mutual support if the U.S. entered the war.

13. Japan negotiated a neutrality pact with Russia in the spring of 1941. At the time Russia was a passive partner to Germany.

14. In 1941 discussions with Japan, the U.S. told Japan to withdraw from China. The talks failed, and the U.S. imposed a ban on all trade with Japan. On December 7, 1941, Japan carried out a surprise attack against the U.S. Four days later Hitler declared war on the United States.

World Figures

Check students' knowledge of world figures during World War II with this oral quiz. Copy the list of names (in the box below) onto the chalkboard or overhead projector. Instruct the students to number a sheet of paper from 1 to 12. Read aloud the clues for each number below, giving students time to choose and write the name of the correct leader. After all twelve have been read, correct the answers together.

NOTE: For your easy reference, answers have been provided at the bottom of this page.

Harry S. Truman	Franklin D. Roosevelt	Neville Chamberlain
Josef Stalin	Hideki Tojo	Mao Tse-tung
Adolf Hitler	Chiang Kai-shek	Benito Mussolini
Winston Churchill	Francisco Franco	Charles de Gaulle

1. During Spain's civil war he led the Nationalist rebels against the Republican government. From 1939 to 1975 he served as Spain's leader.

2. In 1933 this former lawyer was elected president of the U.S.; he kept the country out of war until Pearl Harbor was bombed.

3. A soldier and journalist before establishing the Italian fascist party in 1919, he allied with Germany at the beginning of World War II.

4. After succeeding Lenin, he became the most powerful man in the Soviet Union by making himself dictator.

5. Britain's prime minister from 1937 to 1940, he pursued a policy of appeasement towards Hitler and Mussolini.

6. After serving as vice president for only four months, he became president of the United States. It was his decision to drop an atomic bomb on Japan in an effort to end the war.

7. This former war minister was Japan's prime minister from 1941 to 1944; he argued in favor of an aggressive expansionist policy.

8. The founder and leader of the Nazi party, he called himself *der Führer*. In 1945 he was finally defeated by the combined forces of the United States, Soviet Union, Great Britain, and other Allies.

9. This French general fled to England when France fell. He became the symbol of the French resistance during the War. After the Normandy invasion, he served as president of the provisional government (1944-1946).

10. He led 100,000 followers on the Long March. In 1949 he created the People's Republic of China.

11. After England's prime minister resigned in 1940, he succeeded to the position and led his country into war against Germany.

12. As dictator he resisted Japanese aggressors. Later, his troops were defeated by Mao Tse-tung Red Army.

Answers:

1.Francisco Franco 2. Franklin D. Roosevelt 3. Benito Mussolini 4. Josef Stalin 5. Neville Chamberlain 6. Harry S. Truman 7. Hideki Tojo 8. Adolf Hitler 9. Charles de Gaulle 10. Mao-Tse-tung 11. Winston Churchill 12. Chiang Kai-Shek

The Holocaust

Millions of lives were lost during World War II, but not all of them were due to combat. When the Nazis came to power in Germany, they began to persecute Jews. Adolf Hitler, in a desire to promote a "master race" of pure Aryans, was determined to wipe out the entire Jewish population. Because many German Jews were economically successful, had good jobs, and owned nice houses, Hitler's misguided reasoning held them responsible for inflation, the Depression, and other German problems. Hitler also believed that the Aryan race was superior and that Jews were polluting it. Many other people believed in this theory, too. In order to eliminate the "Jewish problem," Hitler built walled prisons called concentration camps in Germany, Poland, and Austria.

Some of these prisons were work camps, while others were nothing more than death factories. Prisoners at working camps like Bergen-Belsen and Dachau in Germany made supplies for the German army. On their arrival at a camp, prisoners' clothing and belongings were taken away. Their heads were shaved and numbers were tattooed on their arms for identification. Conditions at these camps were deplorable. Many inhabitants froze to death; others died from disease or lack of food. Some were killed when they were no longer able to work. At the death camps, such as Auschwitz and Treblinka in Poland, prisoners were taken to a shower, but the rooms were locked and pumped full of deadly gas through the shower heads. Later their bodies were burned in huge ovens. In addition, some prisoners were subjected to supposedly scientific testing, surgeries without anesthesia, and gruesome experiments. In all, over six million Jews were killed—that number represented 40% of the world's Jewish population. Additionally, five million disabled, homosexuals, Gypsies, and political opponents of the Nazis were eliminated. The Holocaust was a dark period in history, one that must not be repeated.

Suggested Activities

Research Research and discuss any of the following questions: When and how were the camps liberated? Why wasn't more done by other countries to alleviate the situation? What were the results of the Nuremberg Trials?

References

Never to Forget: The Jews of the Holocaust by Milton Meltzer (HarperCollins, 1976).

Smoke and Ashes: The Story of the Holocaust by Barbara Rogasky (Holiday, 1988).

Anne Frank by Richard Tames (Franklin Watts, 1989).

(Numerous books and articles exist on this topic.)

Teacher Note: The movie *Schindler's List* is also recommended. You will need to get school-district and parent permission in writing before showing this film as the movie is R-rated.

Jackie Robinson

Until the 1940s the American and National Baseball Leagues were closed to African American players. They played in separate leagues, called "Negro Leagues," which did not enjoy the same monetary rewards or respect that the all-white leagues did. In 1946 all of that began to change when the Brooklyn Dodgers signed Jackie Robinson to the team.

Jackie Roosevelt Robinson was born in Cairo, Georgia, in 1919. He was only one year old when his father deserted him, his four siblings, and their mother. The family moved to Pasadena, California, where Robinson attended high school, Pasadena Junior College (now Pasadena City College), and UCLA. At UCLA, Robinson was the first student athlete to letter in four different sports: baseball, basketball, football, and track. As talented as he was, he was forced to quit UCLA in his third year to help support his family. During this time, World War II broke out, and Robinson was drafted into the Army.

Jackie Robinson

After returning to civilian life, Robinson signed on to play baseball for the Kansas City Monarchs of the National Negro League. When Branch Rickey, president of the Brooklyn Dodgers, decided to integrate major league baseball, he sent scouts to watch players in the Negro leagues. Jackie Robinson's name appeared on many of the returning reports. In the spring of 1946, Jackie began playing with the Dodgers' top farm team, the Montreal Royals, and by the next year he had joined the Dodgers. It was not an easy transition, as some of his own teammates protested his presence on the team. The Philadelphia Phillies threatened not to play the Dodgers as long as Robinson was on the team. Another team, the St. Louis Cardinals, threatened to strike. Ford Frick, president of the National League, quickly stopped the protests by promising to suspend any team that participated in a strike. In his first year with the Dodgers, Robinson hit .297, scored 125 runs, and led the league in stolen bases. That year the Dodgers won the National League Pennant for the first time since 1941. In 1947 Jackie Robinson became the first African American to play in the World Series and was named Rookie of the Year. Two years later he led his league with a .342 batting average and won the Most Valuable Player Award. In his ten years with the Dodgers, he helped them to six league championships and the 1955 World Series Championship. In 1962, he was elected to the Baseball Hall of Fame.

Suggested Activities

Facts and Figures Tell students to find out what team the Dodgers played in the 1947 World Series and who won.

Comparisons Compare pay, travel, and other conditions in the Negro Leagues with the all-white leagues.

References

Shadow Ball by Ken Burns (Alfred A. Knopf, 1994).

The Forgotten Players by Robert Gardner and Dennis Shortelle (Walker and Company, 1993)

Fifties Overview

- After World War II Korea was divided in two along the 38th parallel. The country was supposed to be reunited after free elections, but the communists, who controlled the North, would not allow the elections to take place. On June 25, 1950, Kim Il Sung directed his North Korean forces to cross into South Korea. President Truman, who was determined to keep communism from expanding into other regions, had the United States lead the United Nations-directed response. Fighting was not easy in Korea and over 33,000 American lives were lost before the war ended in 1953.

- Elsewhere, the Cold War continued, with the United States pledging support to its former Allies. The Soviet Union entered alliances with China and Eastern European countries.

- The nuclear arms race, which began in late 1949 when the Soviets successfully tested an atomic bomb, also continued. The U.S. exploded the first hydrogen bomb, 500 times more powerful than the previous atomic bombs, in 1952. In less than a year the Soviets tested a similar weapon. The threat of these technologies added to the Cold War tension between the U.S. and the Soviets. In America, public and private bomb shelters were built.

- Concerned by the spread of communism in Europe and Asia, some feared it would take over the world and worried about communist subversion in the United States. Senator Joseph McCarthy led the "Red Scare," accusing hundreds of innocent people and ruining their lives. Finally he was condemned by his fellow senators and he quickly lost favor.

- The Supreme Court ruled in 1954 against segregation by race in public schools. In 1955 Rosa Parks's refusal to give up her seat on the bus for a white person sparked the Montgomery bus boycott. The boycott ended a year later with the Supreme Court decision that segregation on buses was unconstitutional. In 1957 in Little Rock, Arkansas, National Guard troops attempted to block the admission of nine black students to a previously all-white school, Central High School. The Guard was removed by an order from the Supreme Court, and 1,000 army paratroopers escorted the students to their high school. The fight for civil rights continued throughout this and the next decades.

- In 1957 the Russians launched the first artificial satellite, *Sputnik I*. American scientists scrambled to compete in the space race.

- Teen idols like James Dean and Marlon Brando were featured in films. Bill Haley's "Rock Around the Clock" heralded a new era in popular music—rock and roll. Buddy Holly, Little Richard, and Jerry Lee Lewis were popular with teens, but Elvis Presley soon eclipsed all of them.

- Television came into more and more homes during the fifties, changing the traditional lifestyle and family structure. People ate TV dinners while perched around the television. New programs depicted ideal family images. Real events could be seen almost as soon as they happened.

- Women were encouraged to stay at home and to take care of their families. Many lived in the suburbs where all the houses were the same.

For Discussion

1. What effect did the space race have on education in U.S. public schools?

2. What were Elvis Presley's contributions to American music?

3. How did television impact the American family?

The TV Generation

Children born in the late 1940s were the first generation to grow up with television. The full impact of this phenomenon would not be seen for many years. On this page you will read about the beginnings of television.

History During the late 1940s some television programs debuted, but they reached relatively small audiences. In 1948, there were fewer than 17,000 TV sets in the whole United States. By the end of the 1950s Americans owned an estimated 50 million sets.

Criticisms Criticism of the new industry came quickly. Some called the TV an "idiot box" or the "boob tube," claiming that many programs had little value. Educators were concerned about the impact of TV on their students and worried that students might skip their homework to watch shows. The amount of violence and sex depicted in some programs was also worrisome to many.

Lifestyle Changes Almost overnight the lifestyles of millions of Americans changed as people stayed up later to watch shows. Some people stayed inside their homes more, leaving their houses infrequently. With the invention of the TV dinner in 1954, some families even began eating in front of the television set.

Impact One important impact of television was the business of TV commercials which brought in over 1.5 billion dollars in advertising money in the early 1950s. Another way television impacted America was in the coast-to-coast programs which allowed people to view firsthand historical events such as political conventions and presidential inaugurations.

A Scandal Quiz shows were popular during the 50s, but *Twenty-One* created the scandal of the decade. Players answered questions, and if they were correct they could choose to keep going. As the questions grew more and more difficult, the prize money grew larger. One contestant, college instructor Charles Van Doren, amassed $129,000 in prize money. In 1958, however, a Congressional investigation revealed that the show was fraudulent and had given questions to Van Doren and others in advance.

Suggested Activities

Movie View the 1995 movie *Quiz Show* for an indepth look at the quiz show scandal of the fifties.

Response Ask for students' responses to this question: What problems facing television viewers are the same today as they were in the 50s?

Debate Choose two groups to debate this question: Who should be responsible for censoring TV programming, individuals (parents) or the government?

Contrast Contrast the current criticisms of TV viewing with criticisms of TV viewing in the fifties.

Survey Have the students keep a survey of their own or their families' television viewing for one week. Tally and compare the results and discuss them in whole group.

An Extraordinary Bus Ride

She has been called the mother of the civil rights movement, but Rosa McCauley Parks does not consider herself to be extraordinary. Born on February 4, 1915, in Tuskegee, Alabama, McCauley had a normal childhood. She grew up on a farm and attended an all-black school in her neighborhood. Her high school education was cut short by her mother's death, but she finished her schooling after her marriage to Raymond Parks. In 1943 she joined the NAACP (National Association for the Advancement of Colored People) and worked with the Voters' League, registering African Americans to vote. Then came the fateful day. The bus ride on December 1, 1955, began as usual. After completing her job as

Rosa McCauley Parks

a seamstress for a Montgomery department store, Parks boarded the bus to go home. As was required, she took a seat in the back of the bus. When all the seats filled up, Parks was asked to vacate hers for a white man who was just getting on the bus. (At that time in Montgomery the law required blacks to sit at the back of the bus and to give up their seats for white people when all other seats were filled.) On this day, however, Parks refused to move. The bus driver stopped the bus and called for policemen who whisked her away to jail. NAACP leader Edgar Daniel Nixon posted her bail and determined that Rosa Parks would be the last African American arrested for such an action.

Along with other black leaders, including Dr. Martin Luther King, Jr., Nixon declared a one-day boycott of all city buses. Leaflets announcing the boycott were distributed throughout the city, and on the appointed day the results were dramatic. Not one African American rode on any buses there. Because it was such a success, the boycott was extended indefinitely.

For their actions blacks were harassed on the street, hundreds of their leaders were arrested, and many lost their jobs. Still, the boycott continued with African Americans turning to alternative methods of transportation, including walking, carpooling, riding bicycles, and even riding mules. The boycott ended when, after 381 days, the U.S. Supreme Court ruled in favor of Rosa Parks and declared Alabama bus segregation laws unconstitutional. It had cost the bus company $750,000 in lost revenues, but the gains in human dignity were *priceless*.

Suggested Activity

Role-Play Group the students and have them write a script for a role-play about Rosa Park's historic bus ride. Let the groups take turns presenting their skits to the rest of the class. For a prepared play, see the book *Take a Walk in Their Shoes* by Glennette Tilley Turner (Puffin Books, 1989).

Sixties Overview

- In his inaugural address John F. Kennedy challenged Americans, especially young adults, to work for change. Many devoted themselves to the cause of social justice by joining the Peace Corps, while others helped register black voters in Mississippi.

- Legislation in the 1950s had provided for school integration. In the 1960s, attention was focused on eliminating discrimination in all public places and in employment, and on guaranteeing the right to vote. Powerful black leaders emerged and gathered their people to demonstrate against the injustices they had been enduring. They waged their campaign with sit-ins, marches, and other nonviolent means but were often subjected to beatings, bombings, and even shootings.

- The new serious attitudes of young people called for a different style of music. Folk singers with acoustic guitars sang traditional ballads. A new group of young folk artists created new songs about current social problems. These "protest" singers, including Bob Dylan, Joan Baez, and Phil Ochs, often appeared at civil rights and antiwar demonstrations.

- Kennedy's assassination in 1963 shocked and saddened the country.

- The new president, Lyndon Johnson, declared an "unconditional war on poverty" in his first state of the union address and guided the passage of a strong civil rights act and an economic opportunity act.

- Attention focused on the Southeast Asian nation of Vietnam where U.S. troops were helping the South Vietnamese in their civil war against the Communist-held North Vietnam. As the war escalated, students and others began to protest the draft and America's involvement in South East Asia.

- By the middle of the decade, many blacks were discouraged by the slow pace of change through nonviolence. New leaders advocated Black Power, and in major cities, frustration often led to violent confrontations, like the 1965 Watts riots. In 1967 alone there were seventy-five race riots. One of the worst was in Detroit, where forty-three people were killed before peace was restored.

- After the assassination of Martin Luther King, Jr. in 1968, race riots broke out in 124 cities.

- Women demanded equal pay for equal work. No longer content to be suburban housewives, they wanted the same career opportunities and choices afforded to men. Betty Friedan led the women's liberation movement and formed the National Organization of Women.

- Migrant workers united under the leadership of Cesar Chavez and protested the unsafe, low-paying conditions of their labor.

- Lyndon Johnson announced that he would not run in the 1968 presidential election.

- Robert F. Kennedy, brother of the late president Kennedy, decided to seek the Democratic Party nomination. After winning the California primary, he was killed by Sirhan Sirhan.

- The Democratic National Convention was marked by violence between antiwar protestors and police. Jerry Rubin's Youth International Party (Yippies), nominated a pig for president. Ultimately Rubin and seven other radical antiwar leaders were arrested and charged with conspiracy in starting the riots.

- Republican candidate Richard M. Nixon narrowly won the election of 1968. He began his term in office by announcing a plan for Vietnamization of the war and the withdrawal of American forces.

Events in Vietnam

The Vietnam War was the costliest and longest war fought in U.S. history. More bomb tonnage was dropped on North Vietnam than on Germany, Italy, and Japan during all of World War II. Over 50,000 American troops died in Vietnam. How did the U.S. become involved in the war and what was the outcome? These and other issues are addressed in the various sections below.

Beginnings During WW II, Japan invaded French Indochina. After the war, the communist Vietminh seized the capital city, Hanoi, and declared the Democratic Republic of Vietnam or North Vietnam. France supported Emperor Bao Dai and helped to establish a new state of Vietnam, or South Vietnam, with a capital at Saigon. The United States recognized the Saigon government. Meanwhile, the French and the Vietminh were at war. In 1954, at the battle of Dien Bien Phu, the French sufffered defeat and withdrew their forces. Under accords drawn at a meeting in Geneva, France and North Vietnam agreed to a truce and future free elections for reunification. Neither side honored the accords, however, and civil war continued. In 1954 the U.S. offered direct economic aid to South Vietnam. The following year U.S. military advisers were sent to train Vietnamese soldiers.

Domino Theory When Kennedy came into office, his predecessor, President Eisenhower, warned him that if the U.S. allowed South Vietnam to fall to the Communists, the next in line would be Laos, Cambodia, Burma, and on into the Subcontinent. This Domino Theory worried Kennedy, and he pledged to help South Vietnam remain independent. U.S. economic and military aid increased. In 1961, 400 army personnel were sent to Saigon to operate two noncombat helicopter units. By 1962 more than 10,000 U.S. military men were in place.

Gulf of Tonkin After President Kennedy was assassinated, President Johnson vowed not to lose Vietnam to communism. On August 2, 1964, it was reported that the USNS Maddox, a U.S. destroyer in the Gulf of Tonkin, had been attacked by North Vietnam. This incident led Congress to pass a resolution allowing the president to use U.S. troops without a formal declaration of war or approval from Congress. The president ordered jets to begin retaliatory bombing of military targets in North Vietnam. In March of 1965, the first ground-force combat units of marines brought the level of U.S. troops to 27,000. By the end of the year there were almost 200,000 American combat forces in Vietnam.

Tet Offensive North Vietnam and its Viet Cong allies launched a huge surprise attack on major cities in the South on January 30, 1968. Because it began during Tet, the Vietnamese New Year, the attack was called the Tet Offensive. The U.S. counterattack was successful, but both sides suffered massive casualties.

Peace Talks Following the Tet Offensive the U.S. halted bombing in Vietnam, and peace talks were initiated in Paris. No agreement could be reached at that time. Early in 1969 President Nixon announced his plan for Vietnamization of the war, and for a gradual withdrawal of U.S. forces. By September of 1969, 55,000 American soldiers had left Vietnam. Secret peace talks between Henry Kissinger of the U.S. and Le Duc Tho of North Vietnam began in Paris in 1970. The talks continued for three years, as did the fighting in Vietnam. Finally, in January of 1973, a cease fire agreement was reached. The U.S. and its allies withdrew from Vietnam in March of that year.

Suggested Activity

Research Have students find out more about the following people and places associated with the Vietnam war.

My Lai Massacre	Haiphong Harbor	POWS
Lt. Calley	Ho Chi Minh Trail	The fall of Saigon
General Wiliam Westmoreland	Laos	Allies of the U.S.
Danang	Cambodia	Allies of North Vietnam

Presidential Quotes

Three presidents were inaugurated during the sixties, and during their terms in office each said words that are still considered important. Read each quote below. On the lines that follow, explain what each one means.

President John Fitzgerald Kennedy

"And so, my fellow Americans, ask not what your country can do for you; ask what you can do for your country. My fellow citizens of the world, ask not what America will do for you, but what together we can do for the freedom of man."–*Inaugural Address, January 20, 1961*

_____

_____

_____

_____

President Lyndon Baines Johnson

"This administration today, here and now, declares unconditional war on poverty in America . . . It will not be a short or easy struggle, no single weapon or strategy will suffice, but we shall not rest until that war is won."–*State of the Union message on January 8, 1964*

_____

_____

_____

_____

President Richard Milhous Nixon

"We have found ourselves rich in goods, but ragged in spirit; reaching with magnificent precision for the moon but falling into raucous discord on earth. We are caught in war, wanting peace. We are torn by divisions, wanting unity."–*First Inaugural Address, January 20, 1969*

_____

_____

_____

_____

The Civil Rights Movement

Civil rights had long been an issue, but not until the sixties did it reach such urgency. Tired of the slow pace of legislative changes, African American leaders emerged and pushed the civil rights movement to the forefront. Listed below are some important 1960s developments in the civil rights cause.

Sit-Ins This nonviolent action was started on February 1, 1960, by a group of four black students who had gone to the Woolworth's store in Greensboro, North Carolina, to buy supplies. When they sat at the lunch counter for coffee, they were told they could not be served. In protest, the group remained seated until the store closed.

Freedom Rides This project protested the segregation of long-distance interstate bus travel. In 1961 a group called CORE (Congress of Racial Equality) announced plans for seven blacks and six whites to begin a Freedom Ride from Washington, D.C., to New Orleans, Louisiana. The bus did not get far before there was trouble. Angry whites beat several riders and set fire to the bus. Nevertheless, several more freedom rides were planned and carried out before the U.S. government initiated very clear rules about integrating bus stations.

March on Washington On August 28, 1963, more than 2,000 buses and thirty special trains had brought a quarter of a million people to Washington, D.C., to protest against discrimination. People of all races and from all over the country traveled to our nation's capital so their voices could be heard. This is where Martin Luther King, Jr., delivered his famous "I Have a Dream . . ." speech.

Mississippi Freedom Summer During the summer of 1964, close to 1,000 students from the North traveled to Mississippi to participate in the Mississippi Summer Project. Bob Moses had planned the event to create a new political party and provide volunteers to register black voters. This angered many whites, and on June 21, three young civil rights workers were killed.

Selma to Montgomery March On March 21, 1965, Dr. Martin Luther King, Jr., began with a group of 4,000 people across the Edmund Pettus Bridge. By the time they reached Montgomery on March 25, they numbered 25,000.

Poor People's Campaign This was Dr. Martin Luther King, Jr.'s, last campaign. In 1968 he had decided to take his cause North to work to eliminate poverty among blacks and whites.

Riots In Los Angeles from August 11–16, 1965, race riots spread throughout the city's Watts area. Sparked by charges of police brutality, National Guardsmen were called in to restore order. During one week in July of 1967, seventy-five race riots erupted in Detroit. Forty-three people died in the conflicts.

Suggested Activities

Changes With the class, discuss what important changes were brought about by the civil rights movement and how the U.S. government helped the cause.

Resource For more information about these issues read . . . *If You Lived at the Time of Martin Luther King, Jr.,* by Ellen Levine (Scholastic, Inc., 1990).

Martin Luther King, Jr.

On April 4, 1968, the world lost one of its greatest heroes of social causes, Martin Luther King, Jr. He was a man who devoted his life to the nonviolent promotion of civil rights, and yet he died a violent death.

King was born in Atlanta, Georgia, on January 15, 1929. His mother was a teacher and his father was a minister. An excellent student, King graduated from high school at the age of 15. He continued his education at Morehouse College and went on to study theology at Crozer Theological Seminar in Chester, Pennsylvania. King later attended Boston University and received his Ph.D. in 1955. While he was in Boston, he met Coretta Scott and they married on June 18, 1953.

For five years during the fifties, King was pastor of Dexter Avenue Baptist Church in Montgomery, Alabama, but he resigned so that he could devote all his time to the civil rights cause. He began to speak out against the discrimination that African Americans were facing. African Americans attended separate and unequal schools, they were forced to sit in the back of buses, and they could not eat at the same lunch counter as whites. It was degrading and unfair, and King was not afraid to speak out about these injustices. After African American Rosa Parks refused to give up her bus seat to a white man, King helped organize the Montgomery bus boycott. King was arrested and jailed, his home was bombed, and threats were made against his life, but he continued his nonviolent protest. As a result, the city changed its segregation laws.

As a student, King had learned about Mohandas Gandhi's technique of nonviolent persuasion for social protest. During a trip to India in 1959, King was able to enhance his knowledge of Gandhi's principles. These were the cornerstone of King's protest.

On August 28, 1963, King led the March on Washington. A quarter of a million people of all races from all over the country traveled to Washington, D.C. to protest discrimination. This demonstration led to the passage of the 1964 Civil Rights Act and the 1965 Voting Rights Act. A charismatic leader and an excellent orator, Martin Luther King, Jr., urged his followers to employ civil disobedience and nonviolent methods of protest. In 1964 he was awarded the Nobel peace prize for his work. It was a fitting tribute to a true hero of the times.

Suggested Activities

Speech Martin Luther King, Jr. was a powerful speaker and is probably best known for his "I Have a Dream . . ." speech. Direct the students to read the complete text of the speech and to write a summary of the important ideas.

Comparisons Compare the lives and works of Medgar Evers and Malcolm X with those of Martin Luther King, Jr. Students can construct a chart or three-way Venn diagram. Alternatively, students can compare King's methods of nonviolence with those of Mohandas Gandhi.

Background Students may be interested to learn what sparked King's dream of equality. Read aloud "Does Friendship Have a Color?" by Valerie Wilson Wesley from the January/February 1996 issue of *Creative Classroom*. Related activities accompany the story.

One Small Step

When President Kennedy was sworn into office in 1961, he vowed to put a man on the moon before the decade was out. Although he did not live long enough to see his dream realized, the nation did witness man's historic voyage to the moon. One of the three astronauts on this momentous mission was Neil Armstrong.

Neil Armstrong

Neil Alden Armstrong was born in 1930 in Wapakoneta, Ohio. During the Korean War he served as a pilot for the U.S. Navy. In 1955 Armstrong graduated from Purdue University and went on to become a civilian test pilot for NASA. At Edwards Air Force Base in Lancaster, California, Armstrong tested the X-15 rocket airplane. When he began astronaut training in 1962, he became the first civilian to join the program. The 1966 Gemini 8 mission was Armstrong's first flight in space. During this flight, he and his partner, David R. Scott, docked their spacecraft with an unmanned spacecraft. After their spacecraft went into a violent roll, the astronauts were able to get the situation under control and safely return to Earth. Three years later, in 1969, Armstrong was chosen to be the commander of the Apollo 11 mission to the moon. Fellow astronaut Edwin E. Aldrin (Buzz) landed and walked on the moon with Armstrong while Michael Collins orbited the moon in the Command module.

As Armstrong made history by becoming the first person to walk on the moon, the world stopped to watch the event on television. On July 20, 1969, Neil Armstrong stepped onto the moon's rocky surface and uttered these famous words, "That's one small step for (a) man, one giant leap for mankind."

After retiring from NASA in 1971, Neil Armstrong became a professor of aerospace engineering at the University of Cincinnati.

Suggested Activities

Moon Map Pair the students and have them draw and label maps of the moon. Instruct them to include the following landmarks: Sea of Cold, Sea of Rains, Sea of Crises, Sea of Clouds, Sea of Moisture, Sea of Nectar, Sea of Tranquility, and the site of the Apollo 11 landing. A great resource for this activity is *One Giant Leap* by Mary Ann Fraser (Henry Holt and Company, 1993).

Debate Ask for volunteers to debate the issue of space exploration. Instruct them to answer this question and provide defenses for their views: Should the U.S. continue to expand its space program or should it be reduced?

Seventies Overview

- The political and social turmoil of the late 1960s continued into the seventies.
- American and South Vietnamese forces entered Cambodia and Laos in 1970 in an attempt to cut North Vietnamese supply lines.
- At Kent State University, students protesting the bombing of Cambodia set fire to an ROTC (Reserve Officers Training Corps) building. Called to stop the riot, National Guardsmen open fire, wounding eight and killing four.
- In a new offensive North Vietnamese soldiers crossed into Quang Tri province, but were stopped by the South Vietnamese. Bombing of North Vietnam by U.S. planes, halted in 1968, resumed in 1972 with railroads and supply lines as principal targets. The harbor at Haiphong was also mined.
- Although peace talks between Henry Kissinger of the United States and Le Duc Tho of North Vietnam began in Paris in 1970, fighting continued until the cease-fire agreement was reached in 1973.
- U.S. troops withdrew from Vietnam in 1973 and from Laos in 1974. In 1975 Saigon fell to the North Vietnamese. The same year, the communist Khmer Rouge came to power in Cambodia, and the Pathet Lao took over the government of Laos.
- In 1971 the publication of the Pentagon Papers, a history of the Vietnam War, added to antiwar sentiments by revealing that the government has not been completely honest.
- A court-martial convicted Lt. William Calley and sentenced him to life in prison for his role in the "My Lai Massacre" of 1968 in which 22 unarmed Vietnamese civilians were killed.
- Early in 1973 the trial of seven men accused of the 1972 break-in and wiretapping of the National Democratic Committee offices in the Watergate building began. Eventually this scandal spread to include members of the president's cabinet and staff and brought the threat of impeachment to President Richard Nixon.
- Spiro Agnew, accused of bribery, conspiracy, and tax evasion, resigned the vice presidency in October 1973. At his trial he pleaded *nolo contendre* and was fined and given probation.
- President Nixon named Gerald Ford, U.S. Representative from Michigan to succeed Agnew. This was the first time the Twenty-fifth Amendment, passed in 1967, was applied.
- In 1974 Richard M. Nixon resigned the presidency. New president Gerald Ford nominated Nelson Rockefeller to fill the office of vice president.
- By 1976 people were quick to embrace Jimmy Carter with his home-spun message of peace and hope as their new president.
- Revelations of misdeeds in government left the activists of the sixties frustrated and disillusioned. They turned their energies inward, embracing fitness, health foods, and transcendental meditation. Some have called the seventies the "me decade."
- Throughout the seventies, the women's movement grew stronger as leaders, including Gloria Steinem and Kate Millet, led the revolution. New opportunities were opened to women and many left the safety of the home to find fulfillment in the workplace.
- In the 1973 landmark Supreme Court decision Roe v. Wade, women were granted abortion rights. A controversial topic, the debate has continued well into the nineties.
- The Arab oil embargo against the Western world had a severe effect on the economy. One effect was a new concern for the environment. Natural foods and fabrics gained popularity, and preventing air pollution and preserving the environment were important growing trends.

For Discussion

How has the women's movement impacted women's lives today?

Does an underlying distrust of the government linger in America today from the Watergate affair?

Is concern for the environment currently a major issue?

The Watergate Affair

On this and the next page you will find a step-by-step explanation of the Watergate affair. Make a copy of both pages for each group of students. After reading the text together, have students complete the activities at the bottom of the next page.

1. The setting is two o'clock in the morning on Saturday, June 17, 1972, at the Democratic headquarters in the Watergate building complex. Five suspected burglars are arrested there. The burglars are attempting to adjust the bugs they had previously installed in order to listen in on Democrats as they planned their strategy for the upcoming election. All five men are wearing surgical gloves and carrying walkie-talkies. Their tools, false identification, telephone tapping devices, money, film, and cameras are confiscated by the police.

2. One of those arrested is James W. McCord, security chief for CREEP (Committed to Re-elect the President). The organization is headed by John N. Mitchell, a former U.S. Attorney General in Nixon's cabinet. Mitchell has resigned that post so that he can manage the president's re-election. He denies any wrongdoing or White House involvement.

3. Two reporters for the *Washington Post*, Bob Woodward and Carl Bernstein, are assigned to investigate the allegations. They find out that the break-in has been directed by G. Gordon Liddy, a former FBI agent, and E. Howard Hunt, a former CIA agent.

4. On August 29, 1972, President Nixon declares that no one in his administration is responsible for Watergate. Furthermore, John Dean, an attorney on his staff, has conducted an investigation clearing all White House staff of any wrongdoing.

5. Nixon wins the 1972 presidential election by an overwhelming majority.

6. On January 8, 1973, with Judge John Sirica presiding, the trial of G. Gordon Liddy, E. Howard Hunt, and the five burglars is underway. Sirica is dissatisfied with the questioning and delays sentencing.

The Watergate Affair *(cont.)*

7. On February 7, 1973, the U.S. Senate creates a Senate Select Committee to investigate Watergate more thoroughly. Sam Ervin, a Democratic senator from North Carolina, is chosen to head the committee.

8. In a written statement, McCord reveals that White House officials had conducted a cover-up to hide their involvement and that they had been pressured to plead guilty while not revealing what they knew. With that revelation, the White House cover-up begins to unravel. John Mitchell admits lying and John Dean, President Nixon's attorney, accuses Nixon's closest advisor of participating in Watergate. H. R. Haldeman, President Nixon's chief of staff, and John Ehrlichman, a top presidential advisor, are also implicated. President Nixon continues to maintain his innocence.

9. On May 17, 1973, televised hearings of Watergate begin. It is discovered that secret audiotape recordings have been made of Nixon and his aides as they conferred about Watergate. At first President Nixon refuses to supply the tapes, but he finally releases some of them. One tape contains an eighteen-minute gap that has intentionally been erased. Another tape made on July 23, 1972, clearly proves that Nixon had conspired with his aides to undermine the FBI investigation.

10. The House Judiciary Committee votes to impeach President Nixon, but he resigns on August 8, 1974, before they can take action.

Suggested Activities

Complete these activities on another sheet of paper. Be prepared to discuss your responses with the other groups in the class.

1. Respond in writing to the following statement: Although the Watergate scandal left the country in great turmoil, it proved that the American system of government works.

2. Watergate can be described as Nixon's worst moment and the event for which he is most identified in history. However, he did take some positive actions. What were some highlights of his presidency?

3. Research and find out what became of Dean, Haldeman, Ehrlichman, and Liddy. Write three or four sentences about each one's career following his incarceration.

Earth Day

The first Earth Day was celebrated on April 22, 1970. Environmentalists conducted demonstrations and rallies across the nation to call attention to the growing problem of pollution. Today, the movement is still growing strong, and there is a bigger commitment than ever to protect the environment and to keep it clean.

On this page are a number of activities you can do to keep the spirit of Earth Day alive all year long. Complete at least two activities from the list below.

Suggested Activities

Learn Keep yourself informed about current environmental issues by reading articles in newspapers and magazines. Share what you have learned with members of your class and family.

Recycle I Think twice before throwing away paper that has only been used on one side. Save it and use it for scrap paper for math calculations, rough drafts, or even for doodling. When both sides have been used, deposit the paper into a recycling bin.

Recycle II Most items can be used a number of ways. Plastic margarine cups are a good example. Clean and save them for food storage, mixing paints, and storing small items such as paper clips. What other uses can you think of? Save other types of plastic, paper, and glass containers and think of new uses for them.

Save Water Be aware of how much water you waste and consume. Take shorter showers rather than baths. Turn the water off while you are brushing your teeth. Remind others in your household to follow the same guidelines.

Conserve To conserve electric lights, dust them regularly. Turn out the lights in a room when you or no one else is using them. In addition to conserving, you will also help your folks save money on the electric bill.

Save the Rain Forest Rain forests play a vital role in the biosphere. In addition to affecting worldwide weather, these forests absorb harmful carbon dioxide and help supply the Earth with oxygen. The rainforests are also our most important source of raw materials for creating new medicines. Help save the rainforests by writing to the Rainforest Action Network, 300 Broadway, Suite 28, San Francisco, CA, 94133. Ask them what you can do to help.

Avoid Styrofoam Styrofoam, or polystyrene foam, is a non-biodegradable material which means that it will never deteriorate—not even if it sits out in the sun or is buried in dirt for five hundred years. As much as possible, avoid using foam cups and plates. Remind your family to purchase eggs packed in paper cartons rather than foam containers.

Read There are plenty of good books out there to help you find ways to preserve and protect the environment. Take a look at *50 Simple Things Kids Can Do to Save the Earth* by The Earthworks Group (Andrews and McMeel, 1990) or ask your librarian to recommend some other titles.

The Amazon Rain Forest

In 1971, construction began in Brazil for a major trans-Amazon highway to open up remote areas of the rain forest for settlement and development. Huge areas of the Amazon rain forest were cut down and burned to make way for about one million new settlers. Because the large cities were so overcrowded and most people were unable to find work there, the government offered lucrative incentives to families who moved to the Amazon. Each family would be given a 240-acre piece of land, housing, and a small salary for a few months. Plans were made to build schools, health facilities, and other services. Thousands made the move but had to give up after only a few months because life in the rain forest was so difficult. The project was deemed a failure.

Not only was the project a failure, but it led to the destruction of a great deal of the Amazon rain forest. The result of this devastation was that much of the rain forest habitat was lost forever and the soil eroded and turned into poor agricultural land. This is indeed a tragedy because the rain forest is so important to the ecology of not only the Amazon but of the world.

Listed below are some ways in which the rain forest is important to mankind. Choose and circle the best response in each parentheses.

1. The rain forest provides (protection/habitats) for many species of plants and animals.
2. When their habitats are destroyed these organisms no longer have a (function/home), and the whole species comes in danger of dying off.
3. More than (200,000/500) different Indian tribes live in the Amazon rain forest.
4. Their (existence/instinct), however, is threatened by the destruction of the land which is their home.
5. Everything that they need—clothing, food, shelter, medicine—can be provided by (resources/animals) found in the rain forest.
6. Western civilization is dependent on the Amazon rain forest for its source of new (medicines/wood).
7. As more and more land is destroyed, many medicinal plants will become (extinct/expensive).
8. Another concern for the Amazon environment is (global warming/fossil fuels).
9. Fossil fuels produce (carbon dioxide/carbon monoxide emissions).
10. Trees are necessary to take in this carbon dioxide and release (oxygen/hydrogen) which is vital to human and animal life.
11. In addition, huge areas of trees like those in the rain forest are important to the (rainfall/water cycle).
12. All of the (grassland/tropical climate) depends on the success of the water cycle.

Answers: Teacher, fold under before copying.

1. habitats 2. home 3. 500 4. existence 5. resources 6. medicines 7. extinct 8. global warming 9. carbon dioxide 10. oxygen 11. water cycle 12. tropical climate

Eighties Overview

- President Jimmy Carter leaves the presidency. On his last day in office, American hostages in Iran are finally released after more than a year in captivity. The release dovetails with the inauguration of President Ronald Reagan.

- Pope John Paul II is shot, but he recovers and gains the admiration of the world by forgiving his attacker. President Ronald Reagan is also shot, and he, too, recovers. A third victim, Indira Gandhi, Prime Minister of India, is shot and killed by her body guards.

- Rock musician, John Lennon, is shot and killed in front of his New York apartment. Millions of fans grieve his loss.

- Britain and Argentina go to war over the Falkland Islands. The United States invades Panama and Grenada and bombs Libyan terrorist bases. Israel forces the PLO from Lebanon. Iran and Iraq go to war. Russia continues its invasion of Afghanistan for nearly a decade.

- A new strategic defense initiative called "Star Wars" gains momentum. The world superpowers agree to reduce nuclear missiles.

- Famine in Ethiopia kills millions. Many make great efforts to relieve the famine, most notably rock musician Bob Geldof and his concert called Live Aid, which earns millions for relief.

- Mikhail Gorbachev comes to power in Russia, bringing about a push toward democracy.

- A nuclear power reactor explodes in Chernobyl, Russia, killing and wounding thousands. The effects of the blast are far-reaching.

- Chinese students in Tiananmen Square protest the government in China. Many are killed by government soldiers who squelch the uprising.

- The Soviet Union begins to unravel, and numerous Soviet bloc countries overthrow communism. The Berlin Wall comes down, and East and West Germany are unified.

- The world's stock markets crash. Insider trading scandals rock the financial world.

- Congress holds hearings over the Iran-Contra affair, uncovering a secret arms deal with American antagonist Iran. Marine Lieutenant Colonel Oliver North admits secretly funneling money to the Contras, an army of Nicaraguan rebels.

- Sandra Day O'Connor becomes the first female American Supreme Court Justice. Sally Ride becomes the first American woman in space. Elizabeth Dole becomes the first woman to head the U.S. Department of Transportation. Geraldine Ferraro becomes the first female candidate on a major party ticket for the office of vice president.

- Technology revolutionizes the American home with personal computers, VCRs, compact disc players, and more.

- Terrorism around the world is on the rise with a number of highjackings, bombings, and hostage situations, most for political reasons.

- A battle against apartheid continues in South Africa and around the world.

- Corazón Aquino is elected Philippine president, replacing President Ferdinand Marcos who is implicated in the murder of Aquino's husband, a former presidential hopeful.

- Human Immunodeficiency Virus (HIV), a retrovirus, is discovered to be the cause of Acquired Immune Deficiency Syndrome (AIDS). The first permanent artificial heart is placed in a patient.

The Berlin Wall

On November 9, 1989, the wall came tumbling down. Here is its history.

Following World War II, Germany was divided, creating Soviet East Germany and West Germany. Berlin, located inside of East Germany, was also divided into East and West zones. In the late 1940s and the 1950s, crossing from East Berlin to West Berlin in Germany became a popular way to escape Soviet communism. Thousands fled Soviet control in this way, and in 1961, more than one thousand East Germans were escaping each day. In order to stop the flight which drained the trained workforce of East Germany, East German police began to construct a wall on August 13, 1961. The wall was made of concrete topped with barbed wire. East Germans continued to escape after the wall was built, but nearly two hundred died in the attempt. Border guards shot them at sight.

The wall became a symbol of the Iron Curtain, the military, political, and ideological barrier that existed between the Soviet bloc and western Europe during the Cold War.

West Berlin itself was constantly under threat of having its supplies cut off. In 1971 Britain, France, and the Soviet Union reached an agreement that provided for free movement between West Berlin and West Germany. As the seventies and eighties progressed, relations between East and West Berlin began to improve.

In 1989 communist governments were failing, and crowds of people were leaving East Germany through Hungary, Poland, and Czechoslovakia. People throughout East Germany were demanding freedom. In November of that year, the East German government succumbed, agreeing to free movement by its citizens. Consequently, the wall that had stood for nearly thirty years was opened. Thousands of people crossed the border within the first few hours of freedom. Citizens began to dismantle the wall any way they could, using picks and shovels and whatever tools were available. People climbed the wall and danced on top, and tourists came from around the world to see the wall come down. Many took home small pieces of it as a reminder of the importance of freedom.

By the end of 1989, communism in East Germany was hanging by a thread. Leaders came and went, and in 1990, communism was voted out. In October of 1990, East and West Germany became a single nation with Berlin as the capital. A few sections of the Berlin wall are still standing and have become outdoor art galleries.

Suggested Activities

Airlift In the late forties, West Berlin was cut off from its supply lines. Research to learn how long the seige lasted and what was done to support the people of Berlin.

JFK John Kennedy was president when the wall was erected. During his visit to West Berlin in 1963, he spoke in German. Find out what he said and explain what it meant to the people of Berlin.

Cartography Draw maps of Germany before and after the unification.

Read Read firsthand accounts of people who witnessed the tearing down of the wall. Newspapers around the world carried the story for weeks.

Write Write a story as though you are an East Berliner present on the day the wall is opened.

Chernobyl and the Exxon-Valdez

In each decade there are sure to be a variety of natural disasters such as earthquakes and hurricanes that strike areas around the world. These disasters often claim many lives and destroy millions of dollars in property. In the eighties, two disasters with far–reaching consequences were caused not by forces of nature but by human error.

The worst nuclear accident ever known occurred on April 26, 1986, near Kiev, Ukraine, which was at the time part of the Soviet Union. One of four reactors at the Chernobyl nuclear power plant went out of control. Due to improper supervision, the water cooling system turned off. This led to an uncontrolled reaction which caused a steam explosion. As a result, the roof was blown off the building, releasing massive amounts of radioactive material into the atmosphere. The radiation easily spread from the eastern Soviet Union to northern and central Europe, causing much concern throughout the area and, in fact, the world. Normal radiation counts jumped to 1,000 times their norm. Farm crops and grazing lands were contaminated as far away as Poland, Scotland, and Great Britain.

According to the Soviets, thirty-one people died immediately of burns and radiation sickness, and more than 300 were injured seriously. However, these numbers are debated elsewhere, and many people believe that they are, in reality, much higher. Medical experts generally believe that there will prove to be an increase in cancer experienced by those closest to the accident. More than 100,000 Soviet citizens were evacuated from the areas surrounding the reactor site.

Three years after the Chernobyl accident, the world's attention shifted to Prince William Sound in southeastern Alaska. An American petroleum company, the largest in the world, the Exxon Corporation, was transporting oil from the Trans-Alaska Pipeline on March 24 of 1989. Its tanker, the *Exxon Valdez*, ran aground and began leaking oil. The leakage continued for two days, spilling nearly eleven million gallons (42 million liters) of crude oil into the water. This was the largest oil spill in North American history. Thousands of marine animals and birds were killed, and 1,100 miles (1,770 km) of Alaska's shoreline were contaminated. Cleanup of the spill cost Exxon approximately two billion dollars. Criminal charges were filed against the company by the United States government in 1990, and in 1991 a plea bargain was accepted. Exxon agreed to pay $1,025,000,000 in penalties and the company pleaded guilty to four misdemeanor charges.

Suggested Activities

Discussion Have the class discuss the following: Is nuclear power worth the risk to life and the environment?

Science Learn about nuclear power and how it is manufactured. Also learn about the uses of crude oil.

Environment What was involved in the cleanup of Prince Edward Sound? What about Chernobyl? Read to find the continuing costs to the environment since the time of both accidents as well as what people are doing (and have done) to better the situations.

Space Shuttles

In the sixties, scientists learned how expensive space travel could be. The expendable booster rockets used to launch satellites for commercial and government use were expensive. A reusable spacecraft, together with launch facilities, mission control, and a system of tracking and data control satellites, would create a new Space Transportation System (STS).

These new spacecraft had to be designed for safety, performance, endurance, and longetivity. There are three components to the shuttle: the orbiter, the external tank, and the solid fuel rocket boosters. The orbiter, which looks like a delta wing fighter, has a wing span of 78 feet (23.79 m) and is 122 feet (37.2 m) long. In its launch phase, it is a stage of a rocket, in orbit it is a spacecraft, and in reentry it is a hypersonic glider. The orbiter contains living space for the astronauts, a large cargo bay, and the engine compartment. The design allows for more crew members than previous spacecrafts and enables the astronauts to bring home large quantities of weighty cargo. There is plenty of room for a variety of work, such as satellite repair, experimentation, the construction of space stations, and deployment of satellites. In theory each orbiter could make one hundred voyages, although the engines would only last through about fifty-five launches. The first orbiter, *Enterprise*, was ready in 1977. It was used solely for drop tests from a Boeing 747 Jumbo Jet, which tested its ability to land after space travel.

An external tank holds cylinders of liquid hydrogen and oxygen to fuel the orbiter's three main engines. Two solid fuel rocket boosters are used to help propel the orbiter to the upper atmosphere. Each one produces 2.65 million pounds (1.20 kg) of thrust.

On April 12, 1981, the first operational shuttle, *Columbia*, piloted by astronauts John W. Young and Robert L. Crippen, went into orbit. They circled the Earth thirty-six times over a period of more than two days. During this flight, the astronauts deployed scientific equipment and ran a variety of tests checking out the abilities of the shuttle.

The sixth shuttle flight in April of 1983 was the first for the orbiter *Challenger*. When *Discovery* was launched in 1984, the crew included Charles Walker of the McDonnell Douglas Corporation, the first person from industry assigned to a shuttle mission. In 1985, U.S. senator Jake Garn flew on the shuttle and took part in medical experiments. The fourth orbiter, *Atlantis*, made its debut for the twenty-first shuttle flight in October of 1985.

Challenger successfully completed nine flights, but on its tenth, the twenty-fifth shuttle mission, in January of 1986, it exploded less than two minutes after take-off. The space shuttle program was halted until the problem could be completely remedied.

The program resumed with shuttle mission twenty-six, completed October 3, 1988 by *Discovery*.

Suggested Activities

Space Flight Learn about other space vehicles of the 1980s, such as *Voyager*. How were they constructed? What did they do? How were they different from those that came before? Also find out about plans for the future of space flight and space exploration.

Read There are many excellent resources about the space shuttle program. Two of them are *Space Shuttle* by N.S. Barrett (Franklin Watts, 1985) and *I Want to Fly the Shuttle* by David Baker (Rourke Enterprises, 1988). Read them as well as others to learn more.

Building Construct models of the space shuttle.

Astronaut Learn about Guion Bluford, the first African American to fly into space. He was the mission specialist on the third flight of the *Challenger*.

1990 and Beyond Overview

- The decade opened with the fall of the Union of Soviet Socialist Republics (U.S.S.R.), followed by restructuring and civil wars throughout the area. Mikhail Gorbachev, the Soviet leader who had been instrumental in bringing about the change, fell out of power and a new era, under the leadership of Boris Yeltsin and others, began.

- War tore apart the nation of Bosnia-Hercegovina, once a part of Yugoslavia, in the aftermath of the Soviet demise.

- Women were on the rise in the United States. The nineties saw the first female attorney general, Janet Reno. Madeline Albright became the first female secretary of state. The position of first lady, the wife of the president, also saw an increased sphere of power and influence in Hillary Rodham Clinton.

- Citizens throughout the United States grieved over the bombing of the Alfred P. Murrah Federal Building in Oklahoma City, Oklahoma, in which 168 people were killed.

- Nelson Mandela, the former political prisoner, became the president of South Africa. Apartheid, the law of racial inequity and separation, ended.

- Hundreds of thousand of black men "marched" to Capitol Hill in Washington, D.C., in a show of solidarity and commitment to racial and family values. Promoters, calling for one million men to join in the march, named the event the *Million Man March*.

- Sports superstars of phenomenal prowess came to the forefront, including the young Tiger Woods who revolutionized the world of golf and brought its appeal to millions of Americans. Also noteworthy were the women's gymnastics, swimming, volleyball, softball, and basketball teams of the United States in the 1996 Summer Olympics. Their record-breaking firsts—and gymnast Kerri Strug's act of heroism—have become legendary.

- The Microsoft Company grew to be one of the most powerful companies in the world under the creative leadership of its founder, Bill Gates, and the revolutionizing Windows program.

- Technology was at the forefront of industry, education, and home life. Everywhere around the world, people were "surfing the net," computing through CD-ROM, exploring virtual reality, and talking on the go via their cellular phones.

- Amid the Israeli-Palestinian peace talks, an assassin killed prime minister Yitzhak Rabin, the Israeli leader at the forefront of peace negotiations. In 1994, Rabin shared the Nobel peace prize with fellow Israeli Shimon Peres and Palestine Liberation Organization leader Yasir Arafat.

- Bill Clinton became the president of the decade with comfortable wins in the 1992 and 1996 elections. However, third-party candidacy was on the rise, largely through the leadership of Reform Party candidate Ross Perot.

- Little green men from Mars were not such an unlikely thing: evidence of life was found on the fourth planet.

- Rap music filled the airwaves while gang-related violence filled the streets. Several of the world's most successful rap stars were gunned down in gang activity, including Tupac Shakur and the Notorious B.I.G. Both were part of the rap movement known as gangsta rap.

The Techno World

Technology in the nineties, just as in the eighties, grew by leaps and bounds. The use of cellular phones and personal pagers became widespread. Not many people, it seemed, were beyond instantaneous reach, and if a person could not be reached by phone, one could always contact him by e-mail.

Here is some detailed information about one of the major technological phenomena of the nineties for those who are a bit less techno-centered.

Internet The term means "interconnected network of networks." It is a wide-reaching system of computers that links businesses and individuals around the globe. Many thousands of individual networks are joined together via the Internet, and the information that can be gained from it comes across in written words, pictures, and sounds.

The history of the Internet can be traced to the sixties. The United States Department of Defense developed a computer linking system for government and military purposes, primarily for security reasons. Shortly thereafter, universities developed a similar network. When the two networks combined, the Internet was formed. Today, anyone with a modem, computer, and Internet software can access the Internet.

The Internet has become one of the most widely used sources of information on any topic imaginable. Internet users can learn about a topic, join in discussions with others, play games, listen to audios, and watch videos. Information may be read "on line" or downloaded to a file or to a printer. The Internet is also used to relay messages from one computer to another. This process is called electronic mail, abbreviated to e-mail.

Modems are used to access the Internet. The modem is connected to the phone line, linking it to the computer. Internet information travels by telephone lines. With the increase in Internet traffic, traditional copper phone lines are being replaced by fiber-optic cables which can transport much more information.

Experts project that the Internet will eventually become a part of the information superhighway, linking computers, telephone companies, cable television companies, financial institutions, and more. Technology for this system is still being developed.

Suggested Activity

Surf the Net In order to use the Internet, you will need the following:

Hardware You will need access to a 386 or faster personal computer or 68030 Mac or Power Mac with at least eight megabytes of random access memory, a 250-megabyte or larger hard drive, and a modem with a speed of at least 14,400 bits per second.

Software Web Browser programs, which permit access to audios, videos and web pages, require a Windows platform. Internet service providers generally supply the software necessary to use their systems, including: e-mail software, Telnet software, Newsreader software, World Wide Web browser, File-Transfer-Protocol (FTP) client software, TCP/IP software, and Gopher client software. As an alternative, software packages like the *Microsoft Internet Explorer Starter Kit* are readily available.

Note to the Teacher : You may wish to install a filtering program which limits access to objectionable material before students begin to "surf." *SurfWatch* from Spyglass is included in some software packages and may be available from your Internet Service Provider (ISP). More information on this program is available at 888-677-9452, or online at http://www.surfwatch.com/index.html.

The Fall of the U.S.S.R.

The decline and fall of the Union of Soviet Socialist Republics (U.S.S.R.) took place over many years.

1985   Mikhail Gorbachev became the Communist Party head, the first of a new generation of leaders. All the old guard leaders had died out.

Gorbachev introduced new policies of openness (*glasnost*) and economic reform (*perestroika*). Books by opponents to communism became available in stores.

1989   The first contested elections in Soviet history were held for the newly formed Congress of People's Deputies. Many top officials lost their positions.

Soviet control over Eastern Europe ended.

There was popular support for reform throughout the eastern region. Many government officials were unseated.

1990   In March, the new office of president of the U.S.S.R. was created, and Gorbachev was chosen. The office replaced the Communist Party head as the most powerful position. Gorbachev also remained as party head.

The Soviet government allowed non-Communist political parties for the first time.

Lithuania declared independence. Estonia and Latvia called for gradual separation from the U.S.S.R. By the end of 1990, all fifteen republics had declared their independence.

1991   To prevent further collapse, Gorbachev negotiated a treaty giving the republics a large amount of independence. Ten nations agreed, and five were scheduled to sign on August 20.

A coup attempt on August 19 preceded the signing. The coup leaders imprisoned Gorbachev and his family. Boris N. Yeltsin, the president of the Russian republic, opposed the coup and helped to end it. On August 21, Gorbachev was released. Yeltsin's prestige increased.

Gorbachev resigned from the Communist Party.

The Soviet parliament suspended all Communist Party activities.

In December, the Commonwealth of Independent States was formed.

Gorbachev resigned as president, and the Soviet Union ceased to exist.

Suggested Activities

History Research to determine what has happened in the former Soviet nations since 1991. Also follow the further career of Boris Yeltsin.

Culture Throughout Communist rule, Russian culture and that of other nations was suppressed. Choose one former Soviet nation and research to find out about its cultural heritage.

End of Apartheid

Background In 1910, former British colonies and two Boer (Dutch) republics formed the Union of South Africa and received dominion status from England. Although whites composed less than 20% of the population, they held all the power, and ruled the country. *Apartheid*, or racial separation, was a common practice in South Africa, but it did not become the law until 1948. When the National Party came to power in 1948, it set up a system called apartheid. The word *apartheid* is from the Afrikaan language of South Africa's Dutch settlers and literally means "apartness." This system kept advantages for white people while limiting those for nonwhites. The policy provided for separate development and eventual independence of the African homelands. The homelands consisted of overpopulated regions with few resources, reserved for 74% of the total population. Independence meant that black Africans had no voting rights in South Africa.

Nelson Mandela

Apartheid Policies Daniel F. Malan of the National Party became Prime Minister of South Africa in 1948. His government defined apartheid policies and divided the population into four groups: whites, people of mixed race, blacks, and those of Asian origin. Public places had separate sections for whites and nonwhites. White students attended separate all-white schools, and railways reserved some first–class coaches for whites only. A later bill required all applicants of color to prove their qualifications in order to vote. More restrictive measures were eventually passed.

ANC The African National Congress (ANC) began in 1912 as a nonviolent civil rights organization. Its purpose was to change the social conditions in South Africa through peaceful protest, dialogue, and education. When more blacks entered the urban work force and apartheid became government policy, membership in the ANC increased, and it became more militant. Strikes, demonstrations and, in some cases, attacks on whites followed. For their part in the uprisings, many ANC activists were imprisoned or executed. One prominent ANC leader, Nelson Mandela, served almost 30 years behind bars for his "crimes."

Second Half of the Century As more African countries joined the British Commonwealth, they pressured Great Britain to force South Africa to abolish apartheid. South Africa refused, however, and left the Commonwealth in 1961 to become an independent republic. Faced with economic sanctions from abroad and violence at home, reform finally began in 1985. Restrictions on the ANC and other political groups were lifted in 1990, and the basic laws of apartheid were repealed in 1991. In 1992 a referendum by white voters approved the end of white minority rule in South Africa, finally ending apartheid. Nelson Mandela became the first black elected as president of South Africa in 1994.

Suggested Activities

Today Research current racial policies in South Africa and prepare a short report.

Mandela Find out about the life of Nelson Mandela and his role in the South African government today.